We Give You Thanks and Praise

Alan Griffiths trained for ordination at the Venerable English College in Rome, where he studied at the Gregorian University and the Liturgical Institute of Sant' Anselmo. He was ordained as a priest of the Roman Catholic Diocese of Portsmouth in 1974.

After a year in parish ministry, he taught liturgical studies at Saint John's Seminary, Wonersh for six years, followed by seven years in campus ministry at Southampton University. In 1994 he was appointed parish priest of the Sacred Heart and Saint Therese Parish, Ringwood.

Fr Griffiths is a member of the Liturgy Commission of his own diocese and of the Pastoral Liturgy Committee of the Bishops' Conference of England and Wales. Since 1986 he has participated in the work of the International Commission for English in the Liturgy (ICEL), a Commission supported by all the English speaking Catholic bishops' conferences worldwide. He was a member of ICEL's Original Texts Sub-committee in the preparation of the new edition of the English version of the Roman Sacramentary, whose collects were published by the Canterbury Press earlier this year.

He is a member of the Advisory Committee of the Institute for Liturgy and Mission of Sarum College, Salisbury. He is currently developing an interest in the building and ordering of churches and ritual spaces, as well as in the works of art and craft commissioned for them.

We Give You Thanks and Praise

The Eucharistic Prefaces of the Ambrosian Missal

Translated by
Alan Griffiths

SHEED & WARD
Franklin, Wisconsin

As an apostolate of the Priests of the Sacred Heart, a Catholic religious order, the mission of Sheed & Ward is to publish books of contemporary impact and enduring merit in Catholic Christian thought and action. The books published, however, reflect the opinion of their authors and are not meant to represent the official position of the Priests of the Sacred Heart.

2000

Sheed & Ward
7373 South Lovers Lane Road
Franklin, Wisconsin 53132
1-800-266-5564

Originally published in 1999 by The Canterbury Press Norwich (a publishing imprint of Hymns Ancient & Modern Limited, a registered charity). St. Mary's Works, St. Mary's Plain, Norwich, Norfolk NR3 3BH

Typeset by Rowland Phototypesetting Ltd,
Bury St. Edmunds, Suffolk
Printed and bound in Great Britain by Biddles Ltd.,
Guildford and King's Lynn

Library of Congress Cataloging-in-Publication Data

Catholic Church.
    [Missal (Ambrosian), Prefaces]
    We give you thanks and praise : the Eucharist prefaces of the Ambrosian Missal / translated by Alan Griffiths.
        p. cm.
    ISBN 1-58051-069-8
        1. Prefaces (Liturgy)—Catholic Church—Texts.
        2. Catholic Church—Liturgy—Texts.
        I. Griffiths, Alan, 1946– II. Title.
BX2015.77 .C38 2000
264´.023´ 094521—dc21
                                            99-046959
                                                    CIP

1 2 3 4 5 / 03 02 01 00

CONTENTS

ACKNOWLEDGEMENTS

After several years' work on the prefaces of the Ambrosian Missal, I still had not thought that any of it would be of sufficient interest to be published. A number of people saw otherwise and advised me to try, in particular Monsignor Anthony Rogers of Our Lady and the English Martyrs' Church, Cambridge, Fr Geoffrey Steel of St Augustine's Church, Preston, Canon Christopher Walsh, Principal of the Institute for Liturgy and Mission, Sarum College, Salisbury, and Miss Elizabeth Lloyd of Liverpool Roman Catholic Diocese Liturgy Commission. In preparing the text I had the help of Mrs Rose Marr of the Portsmouth Catholic Diocese Religious Education Council who read the proofs and of Peter Rafferty who did a monumental amount of photocopying. At the Liturgy Office of the Bishops' Conference of England and Wales Martin Foster put the text on disk and corrected it with me. At the Canterbury Press I met Christine Smith, who accepted the book for publication and helped me through the last stages of the work. Lastly, I thank Bishop David Stancliffe for his interest in the project and for writing the Foreword. I thank my own Bishop, Crispian Hollis, for his kindly encouragement.

FOREWORD

When I first experienced the Ambrosian rite, I was capti-
vated by its style and sound. I had of course known it from
the printed text, but a conference at the Duomo in Milan
gave me a week's exposure to the rhythms of the Office as
well as the Mass. I sought out Canon Inos Biffi who has
overseen the project to translate and represent the
Ambrosian rite in the wake of the reform of Vatican II,
and came away from Milan with three strong convictions.
First, the language and style of the writing reminded me
strongly of the lyric quality of the Syriac hymns of
St Ephraim. The interweaving of rich imagery and biblical
allusions lift the language beyond flatlands and, aided by the
distinctively melismatic chant, allow the worshipper time to
be absorbed into the movement of the prayer. Second, I
was struck by how Anglican the rite felt, both in language,
which felt as if it might have been written by Launcelot
Andrewes, and in liturgical form and presentation. And
third, the lay people I met in parishes as well as in the
Duomo seemed enormously well informed about their dis-
tinctive rite, and proud to belong in the archdiocese with
a history of the unbroken use of a rite with such a claim
to antiquity.

In this important publication, the first of these points is
to the fore, and Fr Alan Griffiths has done the Church a
great service in translating that great treasury of praise
through the Christian Year, the 311 prefaces of the
Ambrosian Missal, and offering them to English-speaking
worshippers. Fr Griffiths is that rare person who combines

deep and reflective liturgical scholarship with a fine sense of English prose and a parish priest's instinct for how these versions will resonate with worshippers.

In contrast to the spare and sober Roman material, the Ambrosian prefaces offer us a richer fare. Vivid scriptural images and memorable expressions of traditional doctrines weave a tapestry, a whole set of icons almost, which set the Church's thanksgiving for what God has done in Christ in context through the seasons of the year. And while this material was conceived as the variable opening to the Eucharistic Prayer, and will be valued as such in traditions other than the rite of Milan where a variable preface is permitted, I can see it forming the basis of other acts of praise in public worship as well in private devotion.

For example, Fr Griffiths cites the new example of the Exultet-like character of the Easter preface, and a number of the prefaces could form the basis of variable Blessings of the Light at Evening Prayer. Others might form Acclamations to herald the new day in place of the hymn at Morning Prayer as in *Celebrating Common Prayer*, or at the end of the Office. Others again might form the basis of an extended meditation on the feast for use the night before or as preparation for receiving communion.

But those who are lucky enough to possess this collection will find many uses for it, and have constant reason to be grateful to Fr Griffiths for his labour of delight and love, which I hope will serve not only to introduce many to the riches of the Ambrosian rite, but also to the possibility of higher standards in the translation of traditional liturgical texts into contemporary English.

David Stancliffe,
Bishop of Salisbury,
Chairman, The Liturgical Commission of the
Church of England.

TRANSLATOR'S PREFACE

Some six years ago I presided at a celebration of Mass in the Ambrosian Rite in the somewhat surprising surroundings of the Southampton University Chaplaincy.

The European Community has schemes for students to exchange across internal borders and so a number of Italian students were coming to Southampton to study such things as Law and Business. Among them were some from Milan.

Good pastoral work at the University in Milan, coupled with (for many of them) the example and teaching of their Cardinal Archbishop, had given these young men and women a good grounding in the faith. In addition, they showed an awareness of and pride in their own local Church which impressed me.

In December 1993 they arranged for a celebration of Mass and a party before they returned to Italy for Christmas. They chose the 7th of December because it was 'their' feast day: the anniversary of that day when, in 387 AD, Saint Ambrose was ordained as Bishop of the Milanese Church.

I possessed a copy of the Italian version of the Missal, and we had the Mass. I had been interested in the texts of the Ambrosian Rite for some time and my encounter with some of its practitioners increased my interest. Friends in Milan obtained a copy of the Latin Missal and I started translating the prefaces. Years passed and I revised earlier work, tinkered with texts and made new versions. The file thickened.

About a year ago I decided, with the encouragement of

some colleagues, to see if anyone would be interested in publishing the collection. To my surprise and delight, the Canterbury Press thought it a worthwhile project. So here it is.

The aim in producing this collection has been to make these prefaces available in English in a translation that is as faithful as I can make it to the original Latin, translated with the help of the Italian text. As far as this primary aim is allowed, I wanted to attempt a version that could be spoken liturgically, so that those whose church customs permit might be able to use the texts as eucharistic prefaces without too much alteration.

I am no scholar and this is not a scholar's edition. Readers will probably not have the Latin or Italian by them so they will have to take much of the work on trust. However, I am convinced that these texts offer a liturgical resource of significance and value. They ought to enrich many people's experience of worship. They have offered me a constant source of reflection on what we believe about the wonderful works of God and how we express that faith.

Liturgical speech constructs and evokes a world of imagery akin to poetry or saga. It is theological but in a new and imaginative way. It is like an ikon in words, a hymn in prose. This is particularly true of the eucharistic preface, for here we not only say what we have to be thankful for but also say it with a loosened tongue and liberated imagination. The prefaces combine scripture and tradition in the richest of colours. It is eventually no surprise to find that the cherubim and seraphim are singing the same song.

Even in the rather pedestrian versions I have been able to produce I hope these texts will elicit interest among those who use liturgical text and those who write it.

Despite the routine and that frequent sense that the right word or expression has just escaped the pen, I found this project immensely exciting. Moments such as the discovery of the Easter Sunday preface were occasions of delight. My only regret is that I have not been able to do entire justice to the wonderful content of these texts.

If readers get as much out of them as has the translator, then I shall be thankful.

Alan Griffiths
January 1999

INTRODUCTION

The Ambrosian Liturgy

For many people and certainly for its own citizens, Milan is the first city of Italy and one of the great cities of Europe. Its modern pre-eminence in manufacturing and the arts is the latest expression of its importance throughout history as a strategic, governmental and cultural centre. Its citizens are hugely proud of their inheritance.

The Church of Milan too has always held its head high in the association of Latin speaking churches in communion with one another and with the See of Rome. The Roman Church this century has taken two of Milan's Archbishops, Achille Ratti and Giovanni Battista Montini, and made them Pope as Pius XI and Paul VI. The present Archbishop, Cardinal Carlo Maria Martini, is a distinguished pastor, scholar and author.

The Church of Milan has its own liturgy. This is one of the few surviving non-Roman Latin liturgical traditions of Europe and of equal antiquity with its Roman sister. After the Second Vatican Council, the Milanese Liturgy was revised in the same way as was the Roman. The *Missale Ambrosianum* appeared in 1981 and its Italian version five years later.

An English Roman Catholic going to Mass in Milan would recognize the familiar shape of the Mass but would also find differences.

Most noticeably they would see different liturgical colours. Red vestments are used after Pentecost where we are used to green. They would hear the Creed recited after the offertory and sometimes the Sign of Peace at this point too. If they heard Eucharistic Prayer I they would hear many more saints' names mentioned than in the Roman version of that prayer. The words of consecration are longer, incorporating as part of Jesus' mandate 1 Corinthians 11:26.

On some occasions in the year the Milanese Mass uses two eucharistic prayers in style and form quite unlike anything Roman.

The Liturgy of the Milanese Church is known as the Ambrosian Liturgy. It takes its name from the greatest of its early bishops, Saint Ambrose (c.339–397 AD).

Ambrose was Governor of Liguria with his seat at Milan. Still in his mid-thirties, his career had already been distinguished and his rise to power impressive. In 374 AD the Bishop of Milan, an Arian, Auxentius, died. There was the prospect of trouble at the election of his successor. Ambrose attended to try and keep the peace. However, popular acclamation demanded him as Bishop. He was still a catechumen; not ordained, not even baptized. On 7 December of that year he was ordained Bishop. This is still his feast day in the Ambrosian Church.

For twenty-three years he was Pastor of the Church which now bears his name. As a reformer, he brought the city back to the orthodox faith. As a statesman, he railed against the cruelty of emperors, forcing Theodosius to do penance for a massacre. As a teacher, he wrote on the religious life and instructed those preparing for Baptism, including among his converts Saint Augustine whom he baptized at Easter 387 AD. Among his surviving work is the earliest substantial citation of a Latin eucharistic prayer that exists. Ambrose died at Easter 397 AD, one of the great Fathers of the Church.

Ambrose's contribution to his own liturgical tradition is not certain, but his is the name attached to it. Its early sources include sacramentaries of the eighth and ninth centuries, and many of its texts, including prefaces, are much older than that.

As a liturgical tradition, the Ambrosian Liturgy is related closely to the Roman. Many texts are common to both. In our own day, the postconciliar reform of the Ambrosian Missal includes many of the prefaces created for the Roman reform.

However, elements of Ambrosian speaking style and textual content point to an early connection with the liturgies of Gaul and the Iberian Peninsula. Influences from the east are also visible.

Today, the Ambrosian Liturgy is used in the Diocese of Milan, as well as in parishes and communities further afield, including some in southern Switzerland.

As a Latin, but non-Roman, liturgy, the Milanese Rite has attracted some interest in this country. The liturgist Archdale King gave a full treatment to it in his *Liturgies of the Primatial Sees* of 1957. However, it is rare for individual liturgical pieces to make their way into English.

The prefaces translated here are from the 1981 Latin *Missale Ambrosianum,* the missal revised after the Second Vatican Council. Compared with the 84 prefaces in the 1970 Roman Sacramentary (a much greater number than in the 1962 Roman Missal), the Ambrosian Rite now has 311 prefaces – excluding repeats – disposed as follows: 151 in the Proper of Seasons; 72 in the Proper of Saints; 35 in the Common of Saints; 12 in the Ritual Masses section; 20 in the Masses for Various Needs and Circumstances section; 8 for Votive Masses; and 13 for Masses of the Dead.

Character of the Prefaces

The function of the preface is to open the Eucharistic Prayer with thanksgiving and praise. Indeed, in the Latin tradition, it is this section that gives the whole Eucharistic Prayer its name and character as a prayer of thanksgiving and consecration.

Following the opening dialogue, the preface consists normally of three sections. First is an opening paragraph taking up the theme of thanksgiving from the dialogue's 'It is right to give thanks and praise.' Next comes the seasonal/occasional section and lastly, a conclusion uniting the praise of the Church with that of the angels, leading into the angelic acclamation 'Holy, Holy, Holy Lord.'

The nature of the preface as thanksgiving for the works of God in Christ allows two primary features to emerge and interweave. The preface is both theology and lyrical image. The 'wonderful works of God' are set out in the context of the Christian annual cycle, which gives to each text its particular colour. This refraction of the whole mystery of salvation through the prism of the Church's Year yields a series of texts that relate each stage of that cycle to the core of it, the Paschal Mystery of Christ.

Prefaces are thus able to offer something unique: a whole series of interwoven images of redemption expressed with a lyricism found nowhere else in the prayers of the Mass.

The Ambrosian prefaces owe their character to the diverse ancestral relationships of the Rite itself: the traditions of Rome, Gaul, the Iberian Peninsula and the Christian east. Two examples will suffice. The Epiphany preface celebrates not just the coming of the Magi but the whole event of the revelation of Christ: the Magi, the sign of Cana, the Baptism in the Jordan. It does so in tones quite unlike the sober understatement of the Roman Epiphany preface, which serves as the Epiphany Vigil preface in the Ambrosian Rite. Even more striking is the Easter Day preface, which seems to be inspired by the Easter Vigil Blessing known as the *Exsultet*. The Ambrosian Rite uses the more staid Roman Easter Preface for the Easter Vigil.

The Milanese encounter with Arianism, a force in Northern Italy for a long time after Saint Ambrose, seems to have left on the Ambrosian Rite the impress of a 'high' Christology emphasizing the Divinity of Christ. The Milanese Eucharistic Prayers V and VI display this strongly. It may also be traced in the prefaces.

Christ is central to the narrative of salvation engaged in by the prefaces. Christ is the Creator, come to restore his creation; the Incarnate One who glorifies his human body with Divine life. Related images are those of the repatriation of humanity to Paradise; the Harrowing of Hades (both images found in the Byzantine Liturgy); the unique centrality of Christ's sacrifice among the many sacrifices of humankind.

The stress on the divine nature of Christ allows the prefaces to bring together the themes of creation and redemption, seeing both as actions of the eternal Son and Word of God. Throughout the Advent/Christmas and Lent/Easter cycle this is a recurring theme. Redemption is seen as a unity, both in the sense of a continuous evolving story from Genesis to Apocalypse, and a restoration of creation, together with humanity, to its primal dignity and beauty.

Finally, readers will observe some strong features of imagery and style. The second preface for Sunday 6 of Advent offers a series of antitheses between the Mother of God and Eve, mythical Mother of all the living. The Maundy Thursday preface contrasts the power of the Son of God with his weakness as one arrested and put on trial before an earthly judge.

Such are some of the theological and stylistic character-
istics of this remarkable collection.

Translating the Texts

All translation contains elements of interpretation and
choice and the whole field is very diverse. *Kelly's Keys To The
Classics* (once forbidden literature in schools) purported
to be translations. Curiously like them were some of the
translations of Latin mass texts in some people's missals of
an earlier generation. Often, such word for word translations made little sense. So it is appropriate that translators
give an account of their work and the principles that have
guided it.

In January 1969 the Holy See set out its own criteria for
liturgical translations. In its Instruction *Comme le prévoit*
it commended three basic principles.

First: liturgy requires both speech and listening. Liturgical
speaking is a ritual symbol in itself and not merely a
form of words to convey ideological messages. Therefore
the grammar, syntax and rhetoric proper to individual
languages must be respected and forms that allow clear
speaking and hearing employed.

Second: the unit of meaning is not the individual word
but the texts as a whole. Therefore, context will determine
how individual terms are translated. The same Latin word
may have differing English renderings in different
contexts.

Third: the language of ritual enactment must be both
common usage and yet remain capable of expressing the
sacred. In other words, archaisms and pastiche attempts
to create a 'sacred' language are unacceptable. However,

this must be reconciled with the need for liturgical speech to maintain a character suitable to a ritual act.

Those broad guidelines have governed all translations within the Roman tradition worldwide since the Council. I have tried, with some reservations explained below, to follow them in the preparation of this collection.

Working from the Latin *Missale Ambrosianum,* I had before me also the Italian translation used in the churches that follow the Ambrosian Rite. This I used as a guide. Where the Italian took a particular approach to the Latin, or clarified obscurities in its text, I tended to follow it.

To those familiar with the style of the current English *Roman Missal,* the texts contained in this collection may seem slightly more complex. The sentences are longer and the syntax more elaborate. Two factors may explain this.

The first is the character of the Latin text. In the Source-book on the Roman Missal prefaces published by the Roman Congregation for Divine Worship the point was made that in preparing the Roman texts the Latinity of the sources employed was modified to aid future translators. Because of the character of its tradition, the Ambrosian prefaces are sometimes more elaborate in style, and less modification of source texts appears to have been made, though I had no detailed source list to verify this. I decided that for this collection it was important to pick up as much of the original as possible, even if the result demanded more of the speaker.

The second factor involved in fixing the style of these translated prefaces is that expectations of the translation process itself have changed since the English language edition of the Roman Missal appeared in 1973.

After the Council the English speaking bishops set up the International Commission for English in the Liturgy

(ICEL) to undertake the translation of the new Latin liturgical books into English. ICEL's early translation policy eschewed complex sentences and elaborate syntax and preferred to parallel, rather than to relate, images and ideas. The spareness of its early translations has not been uncontroversial over the years, leading to criticisms that the texts themselves were less than wholly faithful to their Latin originals.

Without wishing to enter that controversy, it is fair to observe that experience of English ritual speaking in the churches of the Roman tradition has allowed a less radical view of translation style to emerge. It is now recognized that a more complex syntax and higher image colour is not a barrier to the effectiveness of a text. Indeed it may enhance it. In ritual speaking, sound, pattern and rhythm need to be considered as well as the words themselves. Accordingly, the second edition of the Roman Missal in English, now approved by English language Roman Catholic bishops' conferences throughout the world, has opted for a richer syntax and greater closeness to the shape and dynamics of the Latin text.

I have tried to reflect something of this in the translations that follow. Over more than five years, many of the texts have been revised several times and I cannot always be sure with such a large collection that a uniform standard has been maintained throughout. Looking at the complete series I do in fact identify some texts where I have tried too hard to keep more of the original detail than might be thought essential in this sort of translation.

In conclusion, it is necessary to identify some conventions followed in the preparation of these texts. They refer to the opening paragraphs.

I employed a more or less literal reconstruction of the highly stylized Latin openings. These openings pick up the final response of the dialogue which begins the Eucharistic

Prayer: *Dignum et iustum est . . . Vere dignum . . .* 'It is right to give thanks and praise . . . It is truly right . . .' This kind of retrieval is standard practice in the ICEL second edition text. It seems to me that here is a case where English actually gains from imitating the original linguistic architecture.

Also retained in the preface openings is a characteristic Ambrosian addition *hic et ubique* 'always, *here* and everywhere to give you thanks . . .'

At the end of the opening passage where the Latin has *. . . per Christum Dominum nostrum,* I have followed the ICEL practice of turning this as '. . . through Jesus Christ our Lord.'

The concluding paragraphs of the prefaces are more varied than those of the Roman Missal. I have attempted to standardize where appropriate, while reflecting also the variety of detail.

What is this Collection for?

Having begun this exercise as a way of enriching my own liturgical library, I should give some good practical reasons for wanting to publish this book.

The primary function of the texts contained in this book is to serve as prefaces in the celebration of the Eucharist, where church regulations allow this. The texts are laid out with this primary function in mind. They would normally be used with eucharistic prayers designed to begin with a variable preface before the *Sanctus.*

They may also be adapted as discrete sections to form part of a longer semi-fixed preface, such as are found in the *Alternative Service Book* and in other sources. They may also be more widely useful as raw material for those who compose eucharistic prayers.

The prefaces are principally texts for thanksgiving. However, their content indicates that they are also to be regarded as instructive, presenting the mystery of faith in a particular form. This fact implies that they may find a role as a resource in composing other texts for liturgical use. Introductory texts, the more formal parts of addresses or homilies and particularly prayers of blessing and praise for morning and evening prayer will also be able to find material in this collection.

Liturgical texts are valuable (and under-used) sources for personal prayer and reflection. Their particular strength is that they offer a series of constantly changing images of redemption day by day within the context of the Church's annual cycle of celebration.

As narratives of thanksgiving rather than deprecative models of prayer, prefaces stand very close to the heart of all prayer in the Christian tradition, as '. . . a sacrifice of praise to God, that is, the fruit of lips that confess his name' (Hebrews 13:15).

Sources for this Book

The Ambrosian Missal was reformed according to the mandate of the Second Vatican Council and published in a first Latin edition in 1981. Its proper Latin specification is as follows.
Missale Ambrosianum iuxta ritum sanctae ecclesiae Mediolanensis ex decreto sacrosanctae oecumenici Concilii Vaticani II instauratum, auctoritate Ioannis Colombo sanctae Romanae ecclesiae presbyter) Cardinalis Archiepiscopi Mediolanensis promulgatum. Marietti, Milan 1981.
The official Italian Edition:
Messale Ambrosiano secondo il rito delle santa Chiesa di Milano riformato a norma dei decreti del Concilio Vaticano II, promulgato dal signor Cardinale Giovanni Colombo, Arcivescovo di Milano. Two volumes, Milan 1986.
The Milan Journal *Ambrosius, Rivista Di Pastorale Ambrosiana* (subtitle until 1987 vol.63) or *Strumento Per Il Lavoro Pastorale*

Nella Chiesa Di Milano (from vol.64, 1988), contains, from vol.47 (1971) to vol.59 (1983) a lengthy and comprehensive series of articles by Monsignor Inos Biffi and others covering the content of the reformed *Missale Ambrosianum.*

Consilium for the implementation of the Constitution on the Sacred Liturgy, Instruction *Comme le Prévoit* of 25 January 1969, in International Commission on English in the Liturgy, *Documents on the Liturgy 1963–1979, Conciliar, Papal and Curial Texts.* Liturgical Press, Collegeville 1982, pp. 284–291.

Gamber, Klaus, *Codices Liturgici Latini Antiquiores.* Freiburg 1968, pp. 262–271, and Supplement 1988, pp. 62–63.

King, Archdale A., *Liturgies of the Primatial Sees.* Longmans, London 1957, pp. 286–456.

Righetti, Mario, *Storia Liturgical* Ancora. Milan 1949, vol. iii pp. 508 ff.

Triacca, A. M., *Ambrosiana, Liturgia,* in *Nuovo Dizionario de Liturgia a cure di D. Sartore ed A. Triacca.* Ed Paoline, Milan 1983, pp. 16–52.

Ward SM, Anthony and Johnson OSB, Cuthbert, *The Prefaces of the Roman Missal, a Source Compendium with Concordance and Indices.* Congregation for Divine Worship, Rome 1989.

THE PREFACES

THE SEASON OF ADVENT

Ambrosian Advent has six Sundays instead of our four. The focus is twofold: the first coming of Christ in humility and his return in glory. The prefaces of the first and second weeks are repeated in the fourth and fifth. The last week of Advent is a time of more intense liturgical preparation for Christmas, with the final Sunday being celebrated as a feast in honour of Mary, Mother of God.

Sunday 1 of Advent

The Ambrosian and Roman Missals share this preface, created for the Roman Missal in 1968. The text retells the story of salvation around the two comings of Christ.

It is truly right and just, our duty and our salvation,
always, here and everywhere to give you thanks,
Lord, holy Father, almighty and eternal God,
through Jesus Christ our Lord.

When first he came to us
in the lowliness of our human body,
he accomplished the work you purposed long ago
and opened for us the way of eternal salvation;
so that when he comes again in majesty and glory
we may see at last your work completed
and receive the salvation promised us,
which now we await in confidence and hope.

And so, with angels and archangels,
and with all the powers of heaven,
we glorify your holy name
in this, their ageless hymn of praise:

Holy . . .

Monday 1 of Advent (Monday 4)

*Christ's Paschal Mystery is the origin of our salvation. This
preface works that idea into a series of poetic parallels. The syntax
of the Latin text is very condensed, and I have followed the Italian
version's opening out of the preface's structure.*

It is truly right and just, almighty and eternal God,
to give you thanks in all things and for all things,
and to acclaim your wondrous works
through Jesus Christ our Lord.

By coming among us incarnate in human flesh
Christ has brought salvation to a fallen world;
by suffering on the cross
he has redeemed a sinful humanity;
by humbling himself
he has raised our mortality to immortal life;
by being exalted above the heavens
he has made human weakness to triumph
against the power of evil.

And so, with angels and archangels,
and with all the powers of heaven,
we glorify your holy name
in this, their ageless hymn of praise:

Holy . . .

Tuesday 1 of Advent (Tuesday 4)

This very simple thanksgiving has a 'Johannine' ring to it. It is based on the saying of Jesus that he is the Way, the Truth and the Life. Framing this, however, is a specifically Christmas image: the Light has come, putting to flight earth's darkness. Here is the echo of the great Prologue to Saint John's Gospel. Here and elsewhere I have translated the Latin adventus *as 'advent' deliberately, to pick up the seasonal feel.*

It is truly right and just, our duty and our salvation,
always, here and everywhere to give you thanks,
Lord, holy Father, almighty and eternal God,
through Jesus Christ our Lord.

By the advent of his light
he scattered the darkness of this world
and in himself has revealed to us the way of truth
by which we may walk
towards the blessedness of eternal life.

And so, with all the angels we give you glory,
in this, their joyful hymn of praise:

Holy . . .

Wednesday 1 of Advent (Wednesday 4)

Splendour, glory, light; the Cosmos advents on earth; the Creator of heaven's loveliness fills Mary's womb with the same light. For us, in the twenty-first century, there is greater wonder in this image than ever before: we can look at the pictures generated by the Hubble Telescope, showing the glories of God's light in the remotest corners of the universe.

It is truly right and just for us to give you thanks,
to praise and bless you, here and everywhere,
all-powerful and everlasting God.

Your eternal Word
adorned the face of heaven with splendour
and, with the glory of the incarnation,
he filled the Virgin's womb and made it fruitful;
so that a new light in radiant splendour
might shine upon all,
and that from Mary, virgin and mother,
might spring salvation for the human race.

And so, throughout the heavens and the earth
all things adore you and sing a new song;
and we with all the angels give you glory
in this, their ever-joyful hymn of praise:

Holy . . .

Thursday 1 of Advent (Thursday 4)

'From his fullness . . .' With directness and economy this preface once again echoes the Prologue to Saint John's Gospel. In the translation (here and elsewhere) I have retained 'mystery' for Mysterium/a as this is an indispensable part of the Christian liturgical vocabulary.

It is truly right and just, our duty and our salvation,
always, here and everywhere to give you thanks,
Lord, holy Father, almighty and eternal God,
through Jesus Christ our Lord.

From his fullness
Christ has bestowed joy and peace upon all peoples
and by the splendour of his truth
has unfolded the divine mystery of salvation.

And so, with angels and archangels
and with all the powers of heaven,
we glorify your holy name
in this, their ageless hymn of praise:

Holy . . .

Friday 1 of Advent (Friday 4)

This preface takes up the theme of the preface of Advent Sunday 1, but this time with a different emphasis. It is the celebration of the Advent and Christmas Liturgy itself that is presented here as the source of hope and expectation. Christmas is more than a baby in a crib. Faith starts, as it were, in the Nativity cave, but has to look beyond it to the culmination of Christ's work. The role of the Advent Liturgy is to unpack the meaning of the Christmas feast and transform it into longing for the Lord's return.

It is truly right and just, our duty and our salvation,
always, here and everywhere to give you thanks,
and most of all, throughout this Advent time,
to praise you, the Father,
as we look forward to the celebration
of the birth of Christ your Son;
so that as we recall with joy his first coming
we may turn our mind in hope and expectation
to Christ's coming again in glory.

And so, with all the choirs of angels,
we praise your glory, now and for ever
as with one voice we sing:

Holy . . .

Saturday 1 of Advent (Saturday 4)

*Saint Paul's words in Romans 8 about our adoption as children
of God have inspired this preface. From the perspective of Advent
this is particularly appropriate, as the accent here surely lies on
the idea of 'firstfruits' and the hope of glory.*

It is truly right and just, our duty and our salvation,
to give you thanks, always and everywhere, Lord God;
for we have received, from your boundless love,
the firstfruits of your Spirit
to make us even now your adopted children in Christ;
so that bearing our trials with patience
we may look forward to the glory you have promised.

And so, with angels and archangels
and with all the powers of heaven,
we glorify your holy name
in this, their ageless hymn of praise:

Holy . . .

Sunday 2 of Advent

This preface takes up a theme often found in the Ambrosian Rite, that of Christ undoing or reversing the fall of Adam and restoring the likeness of God in the human race. This is expressed through a parallelism: by Christ's human nature our human nature is restored. If this preface sounds more like an Easter preface, that will remind the listeners that Sundays are days of the risen Christ, and Christmas itself a 'little Easter'.

It is truly right and just, our duty and our salvation,
always, here and everywhere to give you thanks,
Lord, holy Father, almighty and eternal God.

You are the source of mercy and compassion,
you desire to pardon sinners, not to punish.
In the human nature of your Son
you have refashioned our humanity
so that death might not henceforth blot out
your living likeness imprinted upon it.
From your own mercy you saved us,
and since through Adam's fall
death had entered the human race,
now in unfathomable love
you have restored that same humanity to life eternal
through Jesus Christ our Lord.

Through Christ the angels praise your glory,
the powers of heaven bow down in adoration;
the cherubim and seraphim together shout your praise.
With these, we pray you, join our voices
in this, their hymn of joyful supplication:

Holy . . .

Monday 2 of Advent (Monday 5)

A preface transforms theology into lyric. This thanksgiving refashions the mystery of salvation as a series of contrasts: slavery and adoption, earth and heaven, mortality and immortality.

It is truly right and just for us to give you thanks,
to bless and praise you, here and everywhere,
almighty and eternal God.

You are the Father of a wonderful compassion
even as you are Lord of an infinite power.
In mercy you have adopted as your children
a people once destined for slavery to sin;
and to those born on earth
into the certainty of dying
you have granted a heavenly birth into eternal life
through Jesus Christ our Lord.

Through Christ the choirs of angels
worship forever with joy before your majesty;
with them, we pray you, join our voices
in this, their hymn of joyful supplication:

Holy . . .

Tuesday 2 of Advent (Tuesday 5)

Advent is a holy time, that is, a time for living more intensely by the strength of the mystery we hold. This preface offers thanksgiving for the call to holiness, using the images of journeying and vigil as its Advent clothing.

It is truly right and just, our duty and our salvation,
always, here and everywhere to give you thanks,
Lord, holy Father, almighty and eternal God.

You offer to your Church these holy days of Advent
to revive and sustain us in hope;
so that we may walk as children of light,
in vigilance and soberness of life,
and come at last to your eternity
with Jesus Christ our Lord.

And so, with angels and archangels
and with all the powers of heaven,
we glorify your holy name
in this, their ageless hymn of praise:

Holy . . .

Wednesday 2 of Advent (Wednesday 5)

The Ambrosian preface collection shows both lyricism and sim-
plicity. In this brief preface, the advent of Christ is paralleled
with Christ's life as a mystery of salvation. The opening lines
echo Psalm 103, 'As a father has compassion on his children . . .'

It is truly right and just, our duty and our salvation,
to bless you, almighty God, both here and everywhere,
because with a father's compassion you have loved us.

Through the advent of the Lord
you have willed to reconcile humanity to yourself
and in the life of Christ
you have brought us salvation.

And so with joy we give you thanks
and acclaim your wonderful works
together with angels and saints
in this, their ageless hymn of praise:

Holy . . .

Thursday 2 of Advent (Thursday 5)

Christmas may be counted as an Easter feast inasmuch as it is a sign of our liberation. This preface asks us to contemplate also the cosmic significance of Christ's coming in language reminiscent of Saint Paul in Romans 8. In the translation I have followed the example of the Italian version and somewhat strengthened this reference.

It is truly right and just, our duty and our salvation,
always, here and everywhere to give you thanks,
Lord, holy Father, almighty and eternal God,
through Jesus Christ our Lord.

By his coming the earth is freed
from all its bondage to decay
and the frailty of our human nature
is loosed from the chains of sin.

Through Christ the choirs of angels
worship forever with joy before your majesty;
with them, we pray you, join our voices
in this, their hymn of joyful supplication:

Holy . . .

Friday 2 of Advent (Friday 5)

In the mystery of the eucharist we say we commemorate Christ's
return in glory. How is this? Here at the altar we defy time and
enter the sacred eternal space of God, even as in the humility of
Christ's birth we defy sense and look upon the glory of his reign.

It is truly right and just, our duty and our salvation,
always, here and everywhere to give you thanks,
Lord, holy Father, almighty and eternal God.

With sacred and solemn rites
we celebrate the coming of Christ in glory,
even as we honour the mystery of his birth.
We recall these great signs of our liberation
resplendent with your marvellous works.

And so, for all your blessings we give thanks
and glorify you with the hosts of angels
in this, their ageless hymn of praise:

Holy . . .

Saturday 2 of Advent

The contrast we saw in the preface of the first Sunday is with us again. In humility Christ came. In majestic glory he is to come again.

It is truly right and just, our duty and our salvation,
always, here and everywhere to give you thanks, O God,
through Jesus Christ our Lord.

Though he is God,
he humbled himself to come among us,
so that he might save from death
those he had created for eternal life;
and he will come again in glory,
bringing the fullness of his gifts
to those whom he has redeemed.

And so, with angels and archangels
and with all the powers of heaven,
we glorify your holy name
in this, their ageless hymn of praise:

Holy . . .

Sunday 3 of Advent

With skill and imagination this preface weaves together two of the great images of salvation from scripture: that of the people making their desert pilgrimage to meet God and Jesus' parable of the Ten Bridesmaids. Both illuminate the celebration of Mass as a journey from Word to Table and, in anticipation, the Banquet of the Lamb. Both turn on the Advent hope, that even before we set out, God advented among us in Christ. Both attest that at the end of all things is the heavenly marriage feast.

It is truly right and just, our duty and our salvation,
always, here and everywhere to give you thanks,
Lord, holy Father, almighty and eternal God,
through Jesus Christ our Lord.

Rejoicing in faith and hope
your Church hastens on its pilgrim way
to greet the advent of Christ the Lord;
until, in the fullness of your kingdom,
she enters with him into the eternal wedding feast.

Through Christ the whole creation gives you glory
and we with the angels also adore you
in this, their ageless hymn of praise:

Holy . . .

Monday 3 of Advent

One of the prayers of the Roman Mass acknowledges that when-
ever the eucharist is offered, the work of our redemption is made
present. This is one of the great themes of early Christian liturgical
consciousness and the idea that animated the modern liturgical
movement. Here it is in preface form.

It is truly right and just, our duty and our salvation,
at all times to praise you, Father almighty,
but most of all to give you thanks at this time
when with abounding joy
we celebrate the advent mysteries of Christ.

Through the flesh of your Son
you bestowed on us the gift of redemption;
now, in this memorial of your loving deeds
that gift is renewed once more
so that we may hold fast the hope we profess
and reign with Christ in eternal life.

And so, Lord God, with angels and all saints
we exult and glorify your holy name:

Holy . . .

Tuesday 3 of Advent

The Old Testament prophets, most notably Isaiah, are an insepar-
able part of the Christmas story. Their theme, that God is faithful
to his promise, is likewise part of the rich texture of Advent
liturgy. These are the 'latter days' – the last times, when we can
see the fulfilment of the promises. This text takes up the words
of Isaiah 7:14, 'The virgin shall conceive and bear a son'.

It is truly right and just, our duty and our salvation,
always, here and everywhere to give you thanks,
Lord, holy Father, almighty and eternal God.

Through the voice of prophets
you promised the coming of your Son in human flesh
and his birth from the Virgin's womb.
Now, in these latter days,
you have fulfilled that promise.
And so with a new joy, we affirm the faith
that Christ has come as our Redeemer
and that he will come again to be our judge.

Therefore with angels and saints
we sing the unceasing hymn of your glory:

Holy . . .

Wednesday 3 of Advent

The theme of exchange is another of the great themes of ancient liturgical text. With wonder and joy the writer of this preface sets it forth here: that God became one of us in order to make us sharers of the very life of God.

It is truly right and just, our duty and our salvation,
always, here and everywhere to give you thanks,
Lord, holy Father, almighty and eternal God,
Creator and Redeemer of the human race.

It was your will and purpose
that your Word should become incarnate
in the womb of the Ever-Virgin Mary,
so that he, your only Son
who came to share our human nature
might wonderfully gather us to himself
as fellow heirs and partakers of the divine life.

And so, Lord God, with angels and all saints
we exult and glorify your holy name:

Holy . . .

Thursday 3 of Advent

The opening words of the First Letter of Peter seem to have been the inspiration for this preface. Saint Peter (1 Peter 1:4) gives thanks for an inheritance 'that can never be spoilt, nor soiled, nor ever fade away, kept for you in heaven'.

The opening and closing paragraph of this preface are strongly in tune with the season of expectation and waiting.

It is truly right and just, our duty and our salvation,
always, here and everywhere to give you thanks,
Lord, holy Father, almighty and eternal God,
through Jesus Christ our Lord
whose coming is soon and without delay.

To those who live by faith
you have granted the consolation
of looking forward to the eternal day of the Lord;
to these you have promised an inheritance
never to be spoilt, never to fade away,
prepared and awaiting them in heaven.

To this glorious heritage we look
and for its joy we keep our heart awake
having on our lips even now
the song of the angels and saints
who praise your glory as they sing:

Holy . . .

Friday 3 of Advent

Again, echoes of the New Testament in this preface, this time Saint Paul. In the Letter to the Romans and in 1 Corinthians Saint Paul parallels Adam and Christ (cf. Romans 5:12–21; 1 Corinthians 15:20–23 & 45–49). The Latin liturgical tradition plays on this parallel, transposing it from a paschal image to a Christmas one, in its portraying of the Incarnation.

In the translation I have added the names of Adam and Christ to make the parallel clear and avoid the repetition of the term 'man'.

It is truly right and just, our duty and our salvation,
always, here and everywhere to give you thanks,
Lord, holy Father, almighty and eternal God,
and to embrace with exultant heart
these holy days of our Saviour's coming.

With boundless love you sent him to us
to become incarnate in our human flesh,
so that, just as through Adam's fall
we fell victim to death,
even so through the victory of Christ
we might rise to new and eternal life.

Therefore with angels and saints
we sing the unceasing hymn of your glory:

Holy . . .

Saturday 3 of Advent

The 'high' Christology of the Ambrosian Rite is manifest in this preface. Though one with us, Christ never separated himself from the Godhead of the Father.

It is truly right and just, our duty and our salvation,
to bless and praise you, here and everywhere.
almighty and eternal God,
through Jesus Christ our Lord
whose advent we eagerly await.

It was his good pleasure
so to enter the Virgin's womb
as both to offer us the way of salvation
and never to part from the majesty of your Godhead.

And so, Lord God, with angels and all saints
we exult and glorify your holy name:

Holy . . .

Sunday 4 of Advent

Creation, fall, promise, hope and redemption, eternal life. This Sunday preface unfolds with elegance and brevity the whole mystery of God's mercy towards us.

It is truly right and just, our duty and our salvation,
to give you thanks, Lord God and Father,
and to celebrate with joy the advent of our deliverance.

Through your eternal Word
you created the human race to be holy,
and when we fell into wickedness
you raised us up in the hope of salvation
by promising the coming of a Redeemer.
In the fullness of time your mercy sent him to us,
so that by sharing our human nature
he might unfold for us your own deepest mystery
and, having released us from the bonds of sin and death
he might raise us up to life eternal.

And so, Lord God, with angels and all saints
we exult and glorify your holy name:

Holy . . .

Sunday 5 of Advent

This preface is repeated as the Thursday preface in the series of prefaces for the days immediately preceding Christmas. Almost breathlessly it lists the reasons for the expectancy and joy of the Advent season. The poetic licence which prefaces enjoy here portrays Christmas as the beginning already of Easter. The 'hope of nations' I have translated as a reference to Christ.

It is truly right and just, our duty and our salvation,
to give thanks to you, the all-powerful Father,
and speak your praises with exultant heart.

Our redemption is drawing near,
the ancient hope of nations is on his way;
the promised resurrection of the dead is at hand,
the glory of your blessed ones already shines forth.

And so, with all the angels we give you glory
in this, their joyful hymn of praise:

Holy . . .

Sunday 6 of Advent

The last Sunday of Advent in the Ambrosian Rite is the Solemnity of the Blessed and Ever-Virgin Mary, Mother of God. Two prefaces are given as alternatives for this day.

The first preface praises the virginity of Mary's conception and birthgiving. The last lines in the Latin are difficult to render in English because they refer to Christ entering and leaving Mary's womb without opening it. Despite the mysterious allusiveness of these lines (some Byzantine hymns may refer to this as an anticipation of Christ's entering and leaving the Upper Room through closed doors on the day of his resurrection) I found it impossible to render this image accurately without sounding either overly medical or merely ridiculous. The version given here attempts to express the spirit rather than the letter of these lines.

It is truly right and just, our duty and our salvation,
to celebrate this feast of blessed Mary Ever-Virgin.

Her womb enclosed, in little space,
the great Creator of the heavens,
and as the Angel had foretold,
she gave birth to the world's Redeemer,
the Word now clothed in human flesh,
the Saviour, conceived and born of her body,
leaving untouched her chaste virginity.

And so, with angels and archangels
and with all the powers of heaven,
we glorify your holy name
in this, their ageless hymn of praise:

Holy . . .

Sunday 6 of Advent

This text is a lyrical reflection on Mary as the Second Eve. From the same root, their common humanity, comes both fall and restoration. Eve is the Mother of all who live, and her inheritance includes Mary, the Mother of God. The complex literary/theological character of this preface makes translation very difficult.

It is truly right and just, our duty and our salvation,
to give you thanks, Lord and almighty God,
and with invocation of your wonderful works
to celebrate the feast of the Blessed Virgin Mary.

From her womb, the fruit has flowered
who fills us with the very bread of angels.
What Eve had lost by her transgression,
Mary has restored for our salvation.
From one motherhood flows a bitter guilt;
from the same motherhood, the advent of the Saviour.
Where once the tempter had prevailed,
now comes a Redeemer as his powerful foe.
From a mortal birth arises the Creator
who leads the human race from slavery to freedom,
and that which was lost to us in our father Adam
is now restored once more by Christ our Maker.

With you, the all-powerful Father
and with the Holy Spirit,
Christ is the praise of angels and archangels,
the acclaim of heavenly powers,
the glory of cherubim and seraphim;
with these, we pray you, join our voices
in this, their hymn of joyful supplication:

Holy . . .

Weekdays before Christmas, 1

In the Ambrosian Rite, as in the Roman, the days before Christ-mas are kept as a more intense period of preparation, contemplating the Nativity of Jesus.

It is truly right and just, our duty and our salvation,
always, here and everywhere to give you thanks, all-holy
   Father,
through Jesus Christ our Lord.

Though he is God,
he came among us in the lowliness of human flesh
so that he might free from death
those he had called to inherit eternal life;
and he is to return in majesty
to bestow the fullness of the kingdom
on those he has redeemed.

And so, for all your blessings we give thanks
and glorify you with the hosts of angels
in this, their ageless hymn of praise:

Holy . . .

Weekdays before Christmas, 2

This preface is found in the Roman Missal as the second of two prefaces for Advent. The Virgin Mary and Saint John the Baptist have a prominent place in the Advent liturgy. This preface honours them by identifying them with the prophets of old.

It is truly right and just, our duty and our salvation,
always, here and everywhere to give you thanks,
Lord, holy Father, almighty and eternal God
through Jesus Christ our Lord.

Christ is the one foretold
in the words of all the prophets;
the child awaited by the virgin mother
with love that surpasses telling;
the one whose coming John foretold
and whose presence he revealed.
Now for the feast of his Nativity
Christ fills us with the joy of expectation,
that his coming may find us ready,
eager and waiting with prayer and praise to greet him.

Therefore with angels and saints
we sing the unceasing hymn of your glory:

Holy . . .

Weekdays before Christmas, 3

There are echoes of the First Letter of Saint John in this preface
(1 John 3:1, 2) for the birth of Jesus is a sign that those who
believe in him are called children of God. Once more, a paschal
note enters the meaning of the Christmas feast.

It is truly right and just, our duty and our salvation,
to give you thanks, almighty Father,
and with the deepest longing of our heart
to await the coming of your only Son.

In your wise providence
the end of all ages draws near to us;
already we are called your children
and that is what we are
for we have received the pledge of our inheritance
which we shall possess openly in its fullness
when Christ the Lord appears in glory.

And so, for all your blessings we give thanks
and glorify you with the hosts of angels
in this, their ageless hymn of praise:

Holy . . .

Weekdays before Christmas, 4

This preface returns to the double sense of Advent, that Christ has come and will return to complete his work.

It is truly right and just, our duty and our salvation,
always, here and everywhere to give you thanks,
Lord, holy Father, almighty and eternal God,
through Jesus Christ our Lord.

At his first coming he restored us to your friendship
and at his return he has promised
to bestow a kingdom for us to possess
in the company of his angels.

And so, Lord God, with all the powers of heaven
we exult and glorify your holy name:

Holy . . .

Weekdays before Christmas, 5

The same preface as for the Fifth Sunday of Advent.

Weekdays before Christmas, 6

This preface is deftly made and in the space of just four lines
encompasses the world that is the Christmas feast.

It is truly right and just, our duty and our salvation,
to give you thanks and praise, Lord God.

Because your mercy has come down from on high,
the Saviour is revealed in human form;
and earth, the home of mortals
receives the eternal King.

And so, with all the angels we give you glory
in this, their joyful hymn of praise:

Holy . . .

Weekdays before Christmas, 7

The same preface as for the Fourth Sunday of Advent.

THE SEASON OF CHRISTMAS

Christmas Vigil Mass

The Ambrosian Liturgy has four Christmas masses: a 'Vigil' Mass for the evening of 24 December, one for the 'Holy Night' of Christmas, one for the Dawn and one for the Day.

At the Vigil, all is anticipation. The 'solemnity of the coming night' is the Midnight Mass. Just visible here too is the Advent theme that as we welcome Christ as newborn, so we welcome his return in glory. So also more of the Incarnation is revealed here in the play on 'visible' and 'invisible', 'eternally begotten' and 'born in time'. This preface has affinities with the Roman Advent II and Christmas II prefaces.

It is truly right and just, our duty and our salvation,
always, here and everywhere to give you thanks,
Lord, holy Father, almighty and eternal God,
through Jesus Christ our Lord.

At this hour we come before him in thanksgiving
and earnestly beseech him
that through the solemnity of this coming night
he may make us watchful in prayer
and fill our heart with welcome
as we celebrate his approaching birth.
For in that birth your invisible divinity
has become visible through a human body,
and he who is one with you,
eternally begotten and equal in Godhead,
has come into this world and is now born in time.

And so, with angels and archangels
and with all the powers of heaven,
we glorify your holy name
in this, their ageless hymn of praise:

Holy . . .

Christmas Night Mass

*'Mild he lays his glory by,/Born that man no more may die,/
Born to raise the sons of earth,/Born to give them second birth.'
Christmas, in fact, is a little Easter. We weave Easter themes into
the celebration of Christ's Nativity. This is the case here. The
opening phrase, 'The birthday not only of the Saviour, but of
salvation', asks the hearers to move beyond the Baby in the
manger to a paschal view of his coming.*

It is truly right and just, our duty and our salvation,
always, here and everywhere to give you thanks,
Lord, holy Father, almighty and eternal God.

Today is the birthday
not only of the Saviour, but of salvation;
since by the birth of Christ your Son
the world itself is reborn,
resurrection is given to the dead
and immortal life restored to mortals.

And so, with angels and archangels
and with all the powers of heaven,
we glorify your holy name
in this, their ageless hymn of praise:

Holy . . .

Christmas Dawn Mass

Early Christian preachers played lyrically with the theme of Incarnation. Theology was less academic in those days and the recovery of such a lyricism for the liturgy of our own times is welcome. This preface uses the metaphor of exchange ('commercium' in Latin) to speak of salvation, and employs healing and medical language to address God.

It is truly right and just, our duty and our salvation,
always, here and everywhere to give you thanks,
Lord, holy Father, almighty and eternal God;
because you have revealed in all its glory
the wonderful exchange that brings us redemption.

Today, from fallen humanity a new humanity arises
and from our mortal nature
comes the cure for our mortality.
Today, out of our human condition
you prepare a healing remedy
when from a race infected by sin
there rises a child who knows no sin.
When your immortal Word
assumes the frailty of our mortal flesh
he gives it a surpassing honour
and through this wonderful union
imparts to us the gift of eternal life.

And so, with all the choirs of angels,
we praise your glory, now and for ever,
as with one voice we sing:

Holy . . .

Christmas Day Mass

This extravagant preface sings the praises of Mary, the Ever-Virgin. If a highlighting of Mary on Christmas Day seems odd, then the content of this thanksgiving will explain it. Mary's role is central to the Mystery of Salvation, inasmuch as she gave human flesh to God. Mary was open to God's bidding and trustful of his purpose. Mary is glorified by the Christmas story. It is the source of her holiness and the reason why she is called blessed.

It is truly right and just, our duty and our salvation,
always, here and everywhere to give you thanks,
Lord, holy Father, almighty and eternal God,
through Jesus Christ our Lord.

The blessed Mary, virgin and mother,
conceived him without impairment of her virginity.
Trusting the promise made her by the Angel,
she bore the Word in whom she had put her faith.
Untouched in virginal honour she remained,
so that she might be called the mother of chastity.
Holy and blessed is the womb of Mary,
who alone among women carried creation's Lord
and for our salvation brought that Lord to birth.

In this therefore let the universe rejoice,
the countless multitude of angels exult,
and let our voices join with theirs
in the unceasing hymn of praise:

Holy . . .

Saint Stephen, First Martyr; 26 December

The preface for Saint Stephen portrays him as one who in suffering death for Christ, also spoke the word of Christ on the cross, commending himself to God and forgiving those who killed him.

It is truly right and just, our duty and our salvation,
always, here and everywhere to give you thanks,
Lord, holy Father, almighty and eternal God,
who called Saint Stephen the Deacon
to proclaim the Gospel of Christ.

He poured out his blood for the sake of your name
as the first martyr of Christ the Lord;
he saw the heavens thrown open
and the Son standing at the Father's right hand.
Stephen took up the words of his Master
and taught, by the shedding of his blood,
what Christ had spoken upon the cross.
Christ the crucified sowed the seed of forgiveness;
Stephen prayed to the Lord for those who stoned him.

Now, as we celebrate his memory
we join the host of angels and saints
in their exultant hymn of praise:

Holy . . .

Saint John, Apostle and Evangelist; 27 December

*The preface for Saint John speaks of his special intimacy with
Christ and his particular insight into the person of the Word
made Flesh.*

It is truly right and just, our duty and our salvation,
always, here and everywhere to give you thanks,
Lord, holy Father, almighty and eternal God,
as we celebrate the memory of Saint John the Evangelist.

The Lord bestowed on John
a lasting place and privilege among his own.
As he hung upon the cross
Christ willed that his beloved disciple
should be a son to his own Mother.
The love with which Christ loved him
transformed him from fisherman to disciple
and gave to him a more than mortal insight
to perceive and proclaim
the uncreated Godhead of Christ the Word.

And so, with your blessed apostle
we join the citizens of heaven
in this, the ageless hymn of your glory:

Holy . . .

The Holy Innocents, Martyrs; 28 December

*This preface celebrates and elaborates the paradox of the Inno-
cents. The children killed by Herod became witnesses to Christ
before they had the power of speech to bear witness.*

It is truly right and just, our duty and our salvation,
to glorify you, the all-powerful Father
for the precious death of these children
murdered by the cruelty of Herod
for the sake of your infant Son
our Lord Jesus Christ.

In them, we acknowledge this great gift of your mercy:
that grace is revealed where strength is least
and martyrdom precedes the power of speech.
The Holy Innocents were put to death
almost as soon as they had been born to life,
and suffered for the name of Christ
before they could profess that holy name.
Truly your goodness is all-powerful and eternal:
they do not know him, yet for Christ they suffer
and you will not let them lose their reward;
but rather, in the shedding of their blood
you enact the saving birth of baptism
and bestow on them the martyrs' crown.

And so, with them and all the choirs of saints
we join the praises of your endless majesty:

Holy . . .

Sunday after Christmas

God is generous, let the Church be abundant in giving thanks.
This preface continues the contemplation of the Christmas mys-
tery as more than just a birthday but a day of new life and
restoration.

It is truly right and just, our duty and our salvation,
always, here and everywhere to give you thanks
and lift our heart to you, the Father,
in honour of this holy mystery
by which our human nature
is set free from its ancient earthly law
and is raised up into a new and heavenly being,
so that what you, our God, in such goodness
have accomplished for our salvation
may be celebrated with unbounded joy
by your exultant Church.

And so, with angels and archangels
and with all the powers of heaven,
we glorify your holy name
in this, their ageless hymn of praise:

Holy . . .

Fifth Day in the Christmas Octave

*The prefaces for Saints Stephen, John the Evangelist and The
Innocents are given in the list of December feasts. This Christmas
preface is found in the Roman Missal as Christmas Preface I. It
is a reflection on the luminous visibility of our God in Christ.*

It is truly right and just, our duty and our salvation,
always, here and everywhere to give you thanks,
Lord, holy Father, almighty and eternal God.

Through the mystery of the Word made Flesh
you have shone with a new and radiant light
upon the eyes of mind and heart,
so that, as we see our God made visible,
we may be caught up in love
of the things that are invisible.

And so, with all the choirs of angels
we join our voice to glorify your name:

Holy . . .

Sixth Day in the Christmas Octave

Christ is the true light; a light not only to the eyes, but also to the mind.

It is truly right and just, our duty and our salvation,
always and everywhere to give you thanks,
Lord, holy Father, almighty and eternal God.

The true light of Christ our Saviour has shone out,
revealing you in glory to our sight
and to our understanding.

And so, with all the choirs of angels
we join our voice to glorify your name:

Holy . . .

Seventh Day in the Christmas Octave

This preface is found also in the Roman Missal, as Christmas Preface III. Like the Dawn preface of Christmas Day, it celebrates the 'exchange' that brought us the life of God.

It is truly right and just, our duty and our salvation,
always and everywhere to give you thanks,
Lord, holy Father, almighty and eternal God,
through Jesus Christ our Lord.

In Christ there has shone forth for us
the wonderful exchange that brings us redemption;
for when your Word takes on our human frailty
our mortal nature assumes immortal honour
and we, through this wonderful union,
are clothed in eternal life.

And so, with all the choirs of angels
we join our voice to glorify your name:

Holy . . .

Christmas Octave Day

This is, in fact, a preface for the Circumcision of Christ. It remem-
bers how Christ was content to fulfil the Covenant of Abraham,
and so to become the maker of the new Covenant. This obedience
mirrors the Incarnation itself, by which he enriches our humanity
with his divinity.

It is truly right and just, our duty and our salvation,
always, here and everywhere to give you thanks,
Lord, holy Father, almighty and eternal God,
through Jesus Christ our Lord.

To redeem us from the burden of the Law
Christ accepted circumcision as the Law required.
In this he affirmed the ordinance of old
and by ridding our former self of sin
he renewed our human nature in his likeness.
Christ has brought to fulfilment
the rites of your ancient saving plan.
By keeping the old Law he gives the new;
by obeying the former precept he teaches a new
    commandment,
since in his fullness as your only Son
he enfolds and enriches the poverty of our human nature.

With you, the all-powerful Father
and with the Holy Spirit,
Christ is the praise of angels and archangels,
the acclaim of heavenly powers,
the glory of cherubim and seraphim;
with these, we pray you, join our voices
in this, their hymn of joyful supplication:

Holy . . .

Second Sunday after Christmas

To our eyes this is a strange text, accustomed as we are to study scripture from the critical point of view only. But the New Testament itself sees a deeper significance to the old narratives, as precursors of Christ. This preface draws on some of Catholic Christianity's most ancient traditional Easter motifs, with the last line to make it a Christmas preface.

It is truly right and just, our duty and our salvation,
always, here and everywhere to give you thanks,
Lord, holy Father, almighty and eternal God,
as we offer to you the sacrifice of praise.

This is the sacrifice begun by Abel the righteous,
and revealed in the Passover Lamb;
the sacrifice made by Abraham
and shown forth by Melchizedek the priest;
the sacrifice brought to perfect fullness
by Christ, true Lamb and eternal Priest
whose birth we celebrate today.

And so, with angels and archangels
and with all the powers of heaven,
we glorify your holy name
in this, their ageless hymn of praise:

Holy . . .

Epiphany of the Lord: Vigil

The Ambrosian Missal provides two masses for this feast, a vigil and a day mass. The Preface for the Vigil Mass is found in the Roman Missal as its single Epiphany preface. It is a simple text celebrating once more the exchange motif, that Christ assumed what was ours (mortality) to give us what is his (glory).

It is truly right and just, our duty and our salvation,
always, here and everywhere to give you thanks,
Lord, holy Father, almighty and eternal God;

Because on this day you revealed
the great mystery of our salvation in Christ,
the light to enlighten all nations;
and now that he has appeared,
incarnate in our mortal flesh,
you have made us anew in the glory
of his immortal life.

And so, with angels and archangels
and with all the powers of heaven,
we glorify your holy name
in this, their ageless hymn of praise:

Holy . . .

Epiphany of the Lord: Day

Like the eastern liturgies which so influenced it, the Ambrosian Mass celebrates at Epiphany more than just the visit of the Magi. The sign of Cana, water changed into wine, is remembered, as is also the Baptism of Christ. Both Roman and Ambrosian Rites have made this last commemoration into a separate feast also with its own texts. This Epiphany preface employs an ending often associated with the Easter prefaces.

It is truly right and just, our duty and our salvation,
always, here and everywhere to give you thanks,
Lord, holy Father, almighty and eternal God,
through Jesus Christ our Lord.

From the moment of his wondrous birth
your eternal Word revealed his power by signs and marvels;
by a star he guided the wise men,
at Cana he changed water into wine,
and at his baptism he made the Jordan's water holy.
By these great mysteries of salvation
we have come to know your purpose
to live amongst us in the person of your beloved Son;
to be for us the way to eternal joy,
the truth in whose light we may clearly see;
the fountain of life that springs up eternally in Christ.

And so, in the joy of this feast,
the earth resounds with gladness;
the angels and the powers of creation
sing with one voice the hymn of your glory:

Holy . . .

The Baptism of Christ

There are two prefaces for this day, and they contrast vigorously.
The first includes a thanksgiving for baptism, the holy waters
that give a new and heavenly birth. The second, found also in
the Roman Sacramentary, is more sober and narrative in tone.

It is truly right and just, our duty and our salvation,
always, here and everywhere to give you thanks,
Lord, holy Father, almighty and eternal God.

In the voice from heaven over the Jordan river
you revealed yourself as the Saviour of all
and the Father of eternal light.
You rent the heavens, blessed the air
and cleansed the springs of water;
then by the holy Spirit in form of a dove descending,
you announced the coming of your beloved Son.
Today the waters have received your blessing
to wash away our ancient curse,
to grant believers forgiveness of sins
and make them your very own children
by a heavenly birth into eternal life.
For, though from our coming newborn into the world
we were subject to death by reason of the fall,
now eternal life receives us
and calls us back to the glory of heaven.

And so, in the joy of this feast
the earth resounds with gladness;
the angels and the powers of creation
sing with one voice the hymn of your glory:

Holy . . .

The Baptism of Christ

Second preface

It is truly right and just, our duty and our salvation,
always, here and everywhere to give you thanks,
Lord, holy Father, almighty and eternal God.

In the waters of the Jordan river
with signs and wonders you revealed a new baptism.
Your voice resounded from the opened heavens
to bring faith that your Word was now dwelling amongst
  us.
Your Spirit descended in the likeness of a dove
to announce that Christ your servant
was anointed with the oil of gladness
and sent to proclaim the good news to the poor.

And so, with angels and archangels
and with all the powers of heaven,
we glorify your holy name
in this, their ageless hymn of praise:

Holy . . .

Weekdays between Epiphany and the Baptism of the Lord: Monday

In our world this time of year is the post-Christmas trough. Having celebrated 'the festive season' since at least the beginning of November, so often the anticlimax begins on Boxing Day. Not so the Church. This preface reminds the assembly that though the feast is past, still the mystery abides and yields its fruit, real and true in the offering of the eucharist.

It is truly right and just, our duty and our salvation,
always, here and everywhere to give you thanks,
Lord, holy Father, almighty and eternal God.

We praise your marvellous works
in these holy days especially
when our heart still resounds
in thanksgiving for the birth of the Lord,
and when that joy, prolonged in sacred rites,
makes us desire the eternal festivity of heaven.
For though the solemn feast day is now past,
still we celebrate the sacred mysteries
that cause your gift of holiness to abide amongst us.

And so, Lord God, with angels and all saints
we exult and glorify your holy name:

Holy . . .

Weekdays between Epiphany and the Baptism of the Lord: Tuesday

In the Roman Sacramentary this is Preface II of Christmas. It plays with the mystery, making a lyrical antithesis: visible/invisible; eternal/of time. The Nativity is presented as an event with universal, indeed cosmic, effect.

It is truly right and just, our duty and our salvation,
always, here and everywhere to give you thanks,
Lord, holy Father, almighty and eternal God,
through Jesus Christ our Lord.

In the mystery we celebrate at this great festival
the One who as God is invisible
has now become visible, appearing as one like us;
the One begotten before all ages
begins to exist in time,
that so, by raising up what was fallen
and restoring creation to wholeness
he might lead a lost humanity
back to the kingdom of heaven.

And so, Lord God, with angels and all saints
we exult and glorify your holy name:

Holy . . .

Weekdays between Epiphany and the Baptism of the Lord: Wednesday

The Ambrosian Rite had to do battle with Arianism: the denial of Christ's Godhead. So it is no surprise to see in this text the orthodox Christology so directly quoted. Dogma, however, is not arid, but woven into a narrative of divine compassion.

It is truly right and just, our duty and our salvation,
to give you thanks, almighty Father,
but at this season more abundantly to praise you
when you have revealed the One
who is the sacrament of our salvation
and the light of the nations.

In Christ your Son we know both God and Man,
who with the fire of love and graciousness
assumed that human nature which is ours
to make us partakers of that Godhead which is his.

And so, Lord God, with angels and all saints
we exult and glorify your holy name:

Holy . . .

Weekdays between Epiphany and the Baptism of the Lord: Thursday

Once again, the Incarnation is set against the background of the Fall, serving thus to present it as the pivot of salvation history.

It is truly right and just, our duty and our salvation,
always, here and everywhere to give you thanks,
Lord, holy Father, almighty and eternal God.

From your saving presence we had been exiled
through the sin of our first parent;
but now in compassionate mercy
you have called us once again to forgiveness and life
by sending to us your only Son, our Saviour.

Through Christ the angels praise your glory,
the powers of heaven bow down in adoration;
the cherubim and seraphim together shout your praise.
With these, we pray you, join our voices
in this, their hymn of joyful supplication:

Holy . . .

Weekdays between Epiphany and the Baptism of the Lord: Friday

The light that has shone out in the coming of Christ not only brings redemption but assures the final hope: that we shall see God as God really is.

It is truly right and just, our duty and our salvation,
always, here and everywhere to give you thanks,
Lord, holy Father, almighty and eternal God.

Most of all, in this holy mystery do we praise you
because the true light of our Saviour has shone forth,
restoring to all of us the life we had lost.
This is the light that shines in splendour
to guide us on our pilgrim way
and lead us to the contemplation
of his glory and boundless majesty.

Therefore with angels and saints
we sing the unceasing hymn of your glory:

Holy . . .

Weekdays between Epiphany and the Baptism of the Lord: Saturday

As the Christmas season moves toward the feast of Christ's Baptism, the theme of illumination (an ancient title of Baptism) comes to the fore.

It is truly right and just, our duty and our salvation,
always, here and everywhere to give you thanks,
Lord, holy Father, almighty and eternal God.

From the farthest days of old
you promised your blessings to us
and now you have made those blessings manifest
through the shining light of Christ our Saviour.

And so, Lord God, with angels and all saints
we exult and glorify your holy name:

Holy . . .

THE SEASON OF LENT

Lent in the Ambrosian tradition functions much like our Lent, that is, it forms a period of six weeks culminating in Holy Week and the celebration of the Paschal Triduum of Holy Thursday, Holy Friday and the Easter Vigil. Those accustomed to the modern Roman Liturgy and its associated traditions in Anglican churches and elsewhere will find much that is familiar.

For example, it is assumed that the parishes will be preparing men and women for Easter Baptism, Confirmation and Eucharist. So growth in faith and the enlightenment given in Baptism is one theme that will recur in the lenten prefaces, particularly in those for the lenten Saturdays.

The celebration of the sacraments of Christian initiation at Easter is heralded on the lenten Sundays by the remembrance of Abraham (Sunday 2), the Samaritan Woman (Sunday 3), the Man Born Blind (Sunday 4) and Lazarus (Sunday 5). These men and women are archetypes. Their experience of coming to faith and the knowledge of God in Christ speaks powerfully both to the candidates for Baptism and the continuing faithful.

Fasting is of course also part of the season and a good number of the prefaces are meditations on fasting and abstinence.

Ambrosian Lent differs from Roman Lent in two particular ways. First, the season begins on the first Sunday. There is no Ash Wednesday in the Ambrosian Liturgy. The Monday following the first Sunday is therefore the first fasting day and the day when the ashes are given (though a rubric allows this to be done at the Sunday mass).

The second difference is that on all Fridays during Lent (not just on Good Friday as in the Roman Liturgy) the Eucharist is not celebrated at all. So there are no preface texts for these days.

Sunday 1 of Lent

At the opening of the Fast, this preface recalls Jesus' words about himself as living bread, food for those who keep the holy forty days.

It is truly right and just, our duty and our salvation,
always, here and everywhere to give you thanks,
Lord, holy Father, almighty and eternal God,
through Jesus Christ our Lord.

In Christ you nourish the faith of those who keep the fast;
you rouse their hope, you fortify their love.
Christ is the true and living bread,
in whom is food for eternal life
and sustenance for righteousness.
Your Word, through whom all things were made,
is the bread, not only of mortals but of angels.
By this bread was Moses your servant
fed for forty days when he received the Law,
fasting so as to desire more keenly your good things.
His body knew no hunger, forgetting earthly food,
because your glory shone upon him
and in the Spirit was he fed upon your every word.
Father, you cease not to give us this bread
that we may ever hunger after Christ Jesus our Lord.

Through Christ the choirs of angels
worship forever with joy before your majesty;
with them, we pray you, join our voices
in this, their hymn of joyful supplication:

Holy . . .

Monday 1 of Lent

The paradox expressed in this preface is hinted at in the preface for the first Sunday. To fast is to feast, Christian spirituality is about feeding on God's word as well as ordinary food so as to acquire strength for works of love and justice. Both eating and fasting are required to live a life pleasing to God. The text ends with a motif that will recur: that through greed we lost God's paradise, so through fasting we must seek it again.

It is truly right and just, our duty and our salvation,
always, here and everywhere to give you thanks,
Lord, holy Father, almighty and eternal God.

You refresh us with bodily food,
but also with food for the spirit,
so that we may live not by bread alone
but by the lifegiving nourishment of your every word.
Thus, not only through eating
but also through fasting, are we sustained and fed.
As you strengthen the body with food and drink,
so through abstinence and works of love
you fortify and renew the soul.
You have consecrated for us this holy fasting season,
to bring us health of mind and body,
so that we may obtain through abstinence
the joy of returning to your paradise
from which we were exiled because of our greed.

And so, Lord God, with angels and all saints
we exult and glorify your holy name:

Holy . . .

Tuesday 1 of Lent

*Christ's fasting, his true hunger for our salvation, his mission to
do the will of the Father (cf. John 4:34) his call to seek food that
lasts (cf. John 6:27) the Word as food (cf. Matthew 4:4); these
themes are skilfully combined in a preface that celebrates the gift
of the holy forty days' fast.*

It is truly right and just, our duty and our salvation,
to give you thanks, most holy Father, here and everywhere,
through Jesus Christ our Lord.

Christ our Lord made this lenten season holy
when for forty days and forty nights
he fasted yet knew no hunger.
For afterwards he hungered
not for the food of mortals but for their salvation;
desiring the holiness of his people
rather than any earthly bread.
For Christ's food is to do your will,
to bring redemption to your people;
and he has taught us to work
not for the food that perishes
but for the lasting nourishment
that is the contemplation of your holy word.

And so, with all the choirs of angels
we join our voice to glorify your name:

Holy . . .

Wednesday 1 of Lent

The Fall of Adam is retold in this preface as a defiance of abstin-ence. It is reversed by the practice of fasting and keeping the commandments.

It is truly right and just, our duty and our salvation,
always, here and everywhere to give you thanks,
Lord, holy Father, almighty and eternal God,
our light and our redeemer.

Through Adam's greed in defying your command
we had been justly cast out of paradise;
now by the remedy of a fast
your grace has prevailed to call us back
to the blessedness of our ancient home;
and your love has taught us the commandments
by which we gain our freedom.

And so, Lord God, with angels and all saints
we exult and glorify your holy name:

Holy . . .

Thursday 1 of Lent

This preface is found also in the Roman Missal as Lenten weekday preface 3.

It is truly right and just for us
to exalt you, the all-powerful Father
and offer you our song of thanks and praise.

You desire us to express our thanksgiving
through works of self denial,
that we sinners may refrain from pride,
and by bringing relief to those in need
may imitate your generous compassion.

Therefore with angels and saints
we sing the unceasing hymn of your glory:

Holy . . .

Saturday 1 of Lent

*The Saturdays of Lent in the Ambrosian Missal have eucharistic
prefaces that celebrate the sacrament of Baptism. This is the first
of them, encapsulating the Paschal Mystery of Christ.*

It is truly right and just, our duty and our salvation,
always, here and everywhere to give you thanks,
Lord, holy Father, almighty and eternal God,
through Jesus Christ our Lord.

By the bodily suffering he endured,
Christ has redeemed the human race;
and by his blood has purified the Church
through the sacrament of Baptism.

Through Christ the choirs of angels
worship forever with joy before your majesty;
with them, we pray you, join our voices
in this, their hymn of joyful supplication:

Holy . . .

Sunday 2 of Lent

Two prefaces are given for this Sunday. The first celebrates the meeting of Jesus with the Samaritan Woman (cf. John 4:1–44). This preface, originally from a Spanish source but found in medieval Ambrosian sources, was included in the Roman Missal after Vatican II for the Fourth Sunday of Lent.

It is truly right and just, our duty and our salvation,
always, here and everywhere to give you thanks,
Lord, holy Father, almighty and eternal God,
through Jesus Christ our Lord.

To reveal the mystery of his coming
in the lowliness of human flesh
he sat down in weariness at the well,
and asked for a drink from the Samaritan woman.
He had already created within her the gift of faith;
now in his compassion he thirsted for that faith
and kindled in her heart the fire of your love.

And so, with angels and archangels
and with all the powers of heaven,
we glorify your holy name
in this, their ageless hymn of praise:

Holy . . .

Sunday 2 of Lent

The second preface given for this Sunday is also found in the Roman Missal as the Preface for Lent 2.

It is truly right and just, our duty and our salvation,
always, here and everywhere to give you thanks,
Lord, holy Father, almighty and eternal God.

You have established for your people a season of grace
to renew and purify their heart and mind;
so that freed from all harmful desires
they may so live in this passing world
as to set their heart on the things that are eternal.

And so, Lord God, with angels and all saints
we exult and glorify your holy name:

Holy . . .

Monday 2 of Lent

Eucharistic thanksgiving continually finds renewed meaning in terms such as 'Redeemer'. In this series of images, Christ becomes our lenten model, resisting the tempter and so making possible the return to paradise for all who believe.

It is truly right and just, our duty and our salvation,
always, here and everywhere to give you thanks,
Lord, holy Father, almighty and eternal God.

You have sent to us from heaven
Jesus Christ your Son, our Lord,
who has opened to us, through his obedience,
the way of return to paradise
from which we were cast out
through eating of the forbidden tree.
By his fast of forty days and nights
he has cast out the tempter
and shown himself as the Redeemer
of all who put their faith in him.

And so, with all the choirs of angels
we join our voice to glorify your name:

Holy . . .

Tuesday 2 of Lent

Abstinence is the gift of a compassionate God, a remedy for pride. As such, it is part of our spiritual sharing in the mystery of redemption.

It is truly right and just to give you thanks,
to bless and praise you, here and everywhere,
God, all-powerful and eternal;
through Jesus Christ our Lord.

You are the compassionate One
who heals our wounded spirit
and washes clean the bruises inflicted by sin.
It is you who cause our fasting to bear fruit
as a remedy for our intemperance and pride.

And so, with all the angels we give you glory
in this, their joyful hymn of praise:

Holy . . .

Wednesday 2 of Lent

*For those who keep it, Lent unfolds a new experience of God's
mercy as they see new Christians preparing for Christian
Initiation, and others making their way through penitence to
absolution. God is always contemporary. Telling of his wonderful
works is a response to knowing those works in our own midst.*

*In translating lines 4 and 5 of the body of the text, I have
expanded the idea of lenten observance, enumerating its traditional features of prayer, fasting and almsgiving.*

It is truly right and just, our duty and our salvation,
always, here and everywhere to give you thanks,
Lord, holy Father, almighty and eternal God.

In your boundless compassion
you give to your people this time of grace
in which the wonders of your mercy unfold before us;
so that through the lenten observance
of prayer, fasting and works of love
we may receive those wonders with thanksgiving
and respond to them with hearts of faith.

And so, Lord God, with angels and all saints
we exult and glorify your holy name:

Holy . . .

Thursday 2 of Lent

Lent speaks not only of Initiation, or of fasting, but of divine forgiveness and reconciliation. This preface is a simple but heartfelt celebration of a merciful and forgiving God.

It is truly right and just for us
to exalt you, the all-powerful Father
and offer you our song of thanks and praise.

In your kindness you absolve the repentant,
you restore to your friendship
the sinner who seeks your forgiveness.
You curb the punishment due for guilt
and with great mercy
you bestow the gift of eternal life.

And so, with all the choirs of angels
we join our voice to glorify your name:

Holy . . .

Saturday 2 of Lent

Sometimes, prefaces parallel the elements of the Mystery of Christ with aspects of our salvation. This is an example. It also employs the image of the Son of God coming down among us to lead us up into heaven, a word-picture often found in liturgical text.

It is truly right and just, our duty and our salvation,
always, here and everywhere to give you thanks,
Lord, holy Father, almighty and eternal God,
through Jesus Christ our Lord:

Whose descent among us has brought the human race
the teaching that saves and sets us free;
whose death has redeemed us from death
and whose rising into glory
has led us into the kingdom of heaven.

Through Christ the choirs of angels
worship forever with joy before your majesty;
with them, we pray you, join our voices
in this, their hymn of joyful supplication:

Holy . . .

Sunday 3 of Lent

Two prefaces are given for this Sunday. The first re-tells the story of Abraham and the divine promise made to him, as this promise is seen through the eyes of Saint Paul (cf. Galatians 3:16) that his 'seed' in the singular means Christ, and that the promise to bless all the nations in his seed is a foreshadowing of the ingathering of the Church 'from every people, tribe and tongue' (cf. Revelation 5:9). This use of scripture, though strange to our rather academic way of understanding it, is based on the fundamental insight that Old and New Testaments alike point to the One God, and the unfolding purpose which finds its fulfilment only in Christ.

It is truly right and just, our duty and our salvation,
always, here and everywhere to give you thanks,
Lord, holy Father, almighty and eternal God.

When you blessed the seed of Abraham long ago,
you foretold in his posterity
the coming of Christ your Son in human flesh;
and that same multitude of nations
which you promised to Abraham as his descendants
you have gathered now
from every people and tribe and language,
and bound them together in the Church of Christ,
in which we rejoice to receive the gift of that blessing
once promised to our holy ancestors.

And so, Lord God, with angels and all saints
we exult and glorify your holy name:

Holy . . .

Sunday 3 of Lent

The second preface for this Sunday recalls the giving of the Law to Moses and the promise of Jeremiah the Prophet (cf. 31:33) that God would write a new law on the heart of his people. This promise is fulfilled in Christ, in whom we are chosen as children of God. In the context of Lent and the preparing of candidates for Easter Baptism, this is a powerful evocation for the Sunday assembly.

It is truly right and just, our duty and our salvation,
always, here and everywhere to give you thanks,
Lord, holy Father, almighty and eternal God.

By the hand of Moses your servant
you committed to your people the ancient Law,
written on tablets of stone;
and now, by the gift of the Holy Spirit,
you have made ready a new law in a new covenant
written upon the heart,
so that men and women
may become your adopted children in Christ,
acknowledging you and calling upon you as their Father.

And so, Lord God, with angels and all saints
we exult and glorify your holy name:

Holy . . .

Monday 3 of Lent

Repentance is a station on the way. Beyond Lent is the light of Easter. God calls his people beyond penance into the sacramental enactment of the Mystery of Salvation and thence at the last to glory, light and gladness.

It is truly right and just, our duty and our salvation,
always, here and everywhere to give you thanks,
Lord, holy Father, almighty and eternal God.

In the observance of these forty days
you call us in your mercy to do penance
so that we may be cleansed of all our faults.
In this way we shall receive the mystery of our salvation,
and, restored to your kingdom of light,
we shall give you joyful thanks and praise.

And so, Lord God, with angels and all saints
we exult and glorify your holy name:

Holy . . .

Tuesday 3 of Lent

This simple preface teaches a simple truth. God longs for his people to return to him.

It is truly right and just for us to give you thanks,
to bless and praise you, here and everywhere,
almighty and eternal God.

You do not seek the death of sinners
but rather the passing of their sinfulness,
and with great mercy and patience
you long for sinners to return to you.

And so, Lord God, with angels and all saints
we exult and glorify your holy name:

Holy . . .

Wednesday 3 of Lent

A journey is hinted at here, a Passover pilgrimage from the sin
we catch so easily from one another towards the day when a new
humanity will be formed.
  The Italian translation adds the lines in italics.

It is truly right and just, our duty and our salvation,
always, here and everywhere to give you thanks,
Lord, holy Father, almighty and eternal God.

With constant loving kindness
you give us your saving help,
so that, turned away from the infection of sin
and living more intensely
the mysteries of Christ our Redeemer
we may approach with eager longing
the day when humanity is made anew.

And so, Lord God, with angels and all saints
we exult and glorify your holy name:

Holy . . .

Thursday 3 of Lent

*The discipline of Lent, prayer and fasting and works of love, are
a spiritual discipline, leading to the rejection of sin and growth
in the divine likeness in which humankind was created.*

It is truly right and just, our duty and our salvation,
always, here and everywhere to give you thanks,
Lord, holy Father, almighty and eternal God,
the fountain of mercy and source of all good.

You call us to keep this holy season,
where through fasting and prayer
and the discipline of your fatherly love
you offer us in Christ a healing for our sins
and the strength to grow in the practice of charity.

And so, Lord God, with angels and all saints
we exult and glorify your holy name:

Holy . . .

Saturday 3 of Lent

In its opening allusion to the illumination of faith, this is a baptismal preface, with a reference also to the Sunday commemoration of the Man Born Blind.

It is truly right and just, our duty and our salvation,
always, here and everywhere to give you thanks,
Lord, holy Father, almighty and eternal God,
through Jesus Christ our Lord.

Christ has dispersed the darkness of this world
with the light of faith,
and through the mystery of the incarnation
has granted sight to a human race born blind
from the womb of its first mother.
He has overridden the just condemnation
which held us in slavery
and has bestowed the grace of adoption
which makes us your beloved children.

Therefore with angels and saints
we sing the unceasing hymn of your glory:

Holy . . .

Sunday 4 of Lent

*On this day the two prefaces provided both recall the healing of
the Man Born Blind (cf. John 9). The first preface interprets the
sign given by Jesus as an image of the healing offered to the whole
of humanity through the sacrament of Baptism.*

It is truly right and just, our duty and our salvation,
to give you thanks and praise, Lord God,
with every power of mind and body,
because through you the blindness of the world is ended
and for those in darkness the true light has shone forth.

Among the brightest miracles of your saving power
you bade the man born blind to gain his sight.
In this you gave us an image
of how the human race,
afflicted from its beginning by blindness,
would receive your healing light
in the sacred waters of Baptism.

And so, with all the choirs of angels,
we praise your glory, now and for ever
as with one voice we sing:

Holy . . .

Sunday 4 of Lent

On the Sunday of the Blind Man, this preface speaks of the redemption of humanity in terms of the Passover journey through Baptism from darkness to light, from slavery to freedom.

It is truly right and just, our duty and our salvation,
always, here and everywhere to give you thanks,
Lord, holy Father, almighty and eternal God,
through Jesus Christ our Lord.

Through the mystery of the incarnation
Christ has led humanity from darkness
to walk in the clear light of faith,
and through a new birth given in baptism
he has adopted as your children
those once born into the slavery of sin.

And so, with all the choirs of angels,
we praise your glory, now and for ever
as with one voice we sing:

Holy . . .

Monday 4 of Lent

The preface is above all 'eucharist' – thanksgiving. It gives the Eucharistic Prayer its fundamental character of openness to God. This preface text captures the essence of all Christian prayer: to thank God for his faithful love, and to express our faith in his continued loving kindness, for 'his mercy endures for ever' (Psalm 136).

It is truly right and just, our duty and our salvation,
always, here and everywhere to give you thanks,
Lord, holy Father, almighty and eternal God.

It is right to glorify you, the Creator of all,
for the fruit of your blessings in the past
and earnestly to beg you for those that are to come;
so that, being found thankful for what we have been given,
we may be judged worthy of what we hope to receive.

And so, Lord God, with angels and all saints
we exult and glorify your holy name:

Holy . . .

Tuesday 4 of Lent

The 'greatest of all mysteries' is the liturgy of Easter, the goal of the lenten observance.

It is truly right and just, almighty and eternal God,
to give you thanks in all things and for all things,
and to acclaim your wonderful works.

With countless gifts of love
you guide your people through these days of saving penance
towards the celebration of the greatest of all mysteries;
so that, by recounting the great deeds
that have brought us to salvation in Christ,
we may be filled with his riches
and be united with him in his passage from death into life.

And so, with all the choirs of angels,
we praise your glory, now and for ever
as with one voice we sing:

Holy . . .

Wednesday 4 of Lent

This is an account of God's love with all the freshness of chapter eight of Saint Paul's Letter to the Romans.

It is truly right and just, our duty and our salvation,
always, here and everywhere to give you thanks,
Lord, holy Father, almighty and eternal God.

You revive us in faith,
build us up in hope
and join us together in your love,
and when our conscience accuses us of guilt
your freely given mercy restores us to innocence.

Therefore with angels and saints
we sing the unceasing hymn of your glory:

Holy . . .

Thursday 4 of Lent

This preface is related to the Weekday Preface 2 of the Roman Missal.

It is truly right and just, our duty and our salvation,
always, here and everywhere to give you thanks,
Lord, holy Father, almighty and eternal God.

In your love
you created the human race without sin;
in your justice
you gave us the due sentence for our transgression;
but in your mercy
you redeemed us from our exile and brought us home.

And so, Lord God, with angels and all saints
we exult and glorify your holy name:

Holy . . .

Saturday 4 of Lent

This is another baptismally inspired preface, with a reminiscence of the previous Sunday's liturgy 'Of the Man Born Blind'.

It is truly right and just, our duty and our salvation,
always, here and everywhere to give you thanks,
Lord, holy Father, almighty and eternal God,
through Jesus Christ our Lord.

Christ has banished from our mind
the darkness of unbelief
and has poured into the human soul
the light of truth and grace;
so that we, once blind in heart,
may acknowledge him as the Son of God
and follow him as the source of our salvation.

Through Christ the choirs of angels
worship forever with joy before your majesty;
with them, we pray you, join our voices
in this, their hymn of joyful supplication:

Holy . . .

Sunday 5 of Lent

On this 'Sunday of Lazarus' the Ambrosian Sacramentary gives two prefaces. The first sees in the raising of Lazarus a depiction of our salvation, and a revelation of Christ's Godhead. As the candidates for Baptism approach Easter, they have, as it were, taken on the identity of the Samaritan Woman searching for faith, of Abraham finding it, of the Blind Man being enlightened and now finally of Lazarus, raised to new life.

It is truly right and just, our duty and our salvation,
always, here and everywhere to give you thanks,
Lord, holy Father, almighty and eternal God,
through Jesus Christ our Lord.

Through signs and wonders upon earth
Christ revealed the glory of his Godhead.
Amid these acts of divine power and love
he raised Lazarus, four days dead,
from the bonds of the grave.
Great is the mystery of our salvation
portrayed in the raising of Lazarus:
the Lord of heaven commands,
and he whose body was dissolved in death
arises straight away into new life.
We also had been buried in the sin of our ancestor Adam,
but now the grace of Christ our God
has freed us from death
and restored us to life in joy that will never end.

And so, with all the choirs of angels,
we praise your glory, now and for ever
as with one voice we sing:

Holy . . .

Sunday 5 of Lent

This second preface is less exuberant than the first, concentrating on Christ's dying and rising as a restoration of a state lost at the beginning of time.

It is truly right and just, our duty and our salvation,
always, here and everywhere to give you thanks,
Lord, holy Father, almighty and eternal God,
through Jesus Christ our Lord.

He died once for all
to establish your grace for ever amongst us;
and by his rising from the dead
he has fashioned anew our human nature,
restoring to us the heavenly gifts
lost through the deceit of the evil one.

And so, with all the choirs of angels,
we praise your glory, now and for ever
as with one voice we sing:

Holy . . .

Monday 5 of Lent

Lent provides the Church with a spiritual discipline of sight readjustment: always to look 'beyond'. To a tradition whose God is utterly transcendent (the quintessence of 'beyond') that is where the eyes must be fixed. We look also to Easter, and to the mysteries by which we are born again.

It is truly right and just, our duty and our salvation,
always, here and everywhere to give you thanks,
Lord, holy Father, almighty and eternal God.

From your gift of this world's goods
you encourage us to discern
the gifts that last eternally.
You grant us the things of earth
and promise us the things of heaven,
so that even now we may begin
to be citizens of your eternal kingdom
and not be held captive by this passing age.
Yours is the gift of mortal life;
and though our nature bears the wounds of sin,
yours is the work by which we are born again
from earthly life into the life of heaven.

And so, Lord God, with angels and all saints
we exult and glorify your holy name:

Holy . . .

Tuesday 5 of Lent

From fasting to forgiveness: the ritual observance of Lent con-cludes in Holy Week with the celebration of forgiveness in prep-aration for Easter. The sense of this preface is that Easter itself will be the gateway of eternal joy.

It is truly right and just, almighty and eternal God,
to give you thanks in all things and for all things
and to tell of your wonderful works.

You ordain that we keep this lenten fast,
to strengthen our hope in your mercy and forgiveness.
You train us to celebrate the paschal feast
so as to find therein a joy that lasts for ever.

And so, with all the angels we give you glory
in this, their joyful hymn of praise:

Holy . . .

Wednesday 5 of Lent

This preface highlights again two of the primary works that constitute Christian Lent: prayer and works of love to gain purity of heart. It is possible to discern in this prayer a hint of Saint John's vision of what it both is, and will be, to be revealed as children of God (cf. 1 John 3:2). This preface is a slightly more elaborate version of one found in the Roman Sacramentary as the Preface of Lent 1.

It is truly right and just, our duty and our salvation,
always, here and everywhere to give you thanks,
Lord, holy Father, almighty and eternal God.

In mercy you call your people to cleanse their heart
and look forward to the yearly paschal feast
so that by abundance of prayer and works of love
and by celebrating the mysteries
through which Christ has granted them a new birth,
your sons and daughters may be brought
into the full stature of your children.

And so, with all the angels we give you glory
in this, their joyful hymn of praise:

Holy . . .

Thursday 5 of Lent

Here is a text on the theme of exchange, such as appears in the Christmas season. Here the image is of God making good from bad, as it were; from mortality itself raising up what is immortal. A version of this preface appears in the Roman Missal as the Preface for Sundays of Ordinary Time 3.

It is truly right and just, our duty and our salvation,
always, here and everywhere to give you thanks,
Lord, holy Father, almighty and eternal God.

Your boundless glory is shown in this:
that by your power as God most high
you came to rescue our mortal nature.
Moreover, from that same weakness of our mortality
you drew forth a healing remedy,
turning that nature which had led to our fall
into the very means of our salvation.

Therefore with angels and saints
we sing the unceasing hymn of your glory:

Holy . . .

Saturday 5 of Lent – The Giving of the Creed

The title of this day refers to the rite of 'handing on' the Creed to those whose Easter Baptism is drawing closer. The preface speaks of the teaching of the faith and the knowledge that comes with incorporation into the body of Christ.

It is truly right and just, our duty and our salvation,
always, here and everywhere to give you thanks,
Lord, holy Father, almighty and eternal God.

This is the time of your special blessing;
you do not cease to enlighten your children
with the good news of their salvation,
and with tireless mercy you come to their aid;
so that in Christ they may learn
to recognize the way of right action
and receive the strength to make it their own.

Therefore with angels and saints
we sing the unceasing hymn of your glory:

Holy . . .

Holy Week – Palm Sunday

The Ambrosian Rite has two masses for Palm Sunday. The first of these is the celebration of the messianic entry into Jerusalem. The Palm Procession takes place before this Mass. The second Mass is a passiontide liturgy. This arrangement of liturgies represents a coming together of two traditions: the messianic entry celebration which relates to other ancient Latin and eastern liturgies, and the Passion celebration, more Roman in tone. However, whereas the Roman Rite developed the pattern of Palm Procession and Passion Mass as one celebration, the Church of Milan elected to keep these two elements separate altogether.

It is truly right and just, our duty and our salvation,
always, here and everywhere to give you thanks,
Lord, holy Father, almighty and eternal God.

You sent your Son, our Lord Jesus Christ,
into this world for us and for our salvation,
so that by the wondrous mystery of his humility
and his acceptance of our mortal suffering,
he might call us back to fellowship with you.
As he entered Jerusalem to fulfil the scriptures
the crowd welcomed him with faith and acclamation,
spreading their garments with olive branches in his way.

Now therefore, as the children sang his praises,
it is right that we also, in love of Christ,
should lift our voice in joyful tribute:

Holy . . .

Holy Week – Palm Sunday

This second preface is for the Passion Mass. It is found in the Roman Missal also as the preface for this day.

It is truly right and just, our duty and our salvation,
always, here and everywhere to give you thanks,
Lord, holy Father, almighty and eternal God,
through Jesus Christ our Lord.

Though he was innocent,
he freely accepted suffering for the guilty
and an unjust sentence on behalf of sinners.
His death has washed away our sins,
his rising has restored us to peace with you.

And so, Lord God, with angels and all saints
we exult and glorify your holy name:

Holy . . .

Holy Week – Monday

This preface offers a panoramic vision of our salvation in the
Paschal Mystery of Christ.

It is truly right and just, our duty and our salvation,
always, here and everywhere to give you thanks,
Lord, holy Father, almighty and eternal God,
through Jesus Christ our Lord.

By the human nature he assumed
he gathers us all into one body;
humbled, he raises us up;
handed over to death, he sets us free.
His suffering redeems us, his cross saves us;
his blood cleanses us, his flesh feeds us.

And so, Lord God, with angels and all saints
we exult and glorify your holy name:

Holy . . .

Holy Week – Tuesday

Also found in the Roman Missal as the second preface of the Passion, this thanksgiving looks forward to the celebration of the mystery of redemption in the Triduum Liturgy.

It is truly right and just, our duty and our salvation,
always, here and everywhere to give you thanks,
Lord, holy Father, almighty and eternal God,
through Jesus Christ our Lord.

The days of his lifegiving death and glorious resurrection
are now close at hand;
when the pride of our ancient enemy is trampled down
and the mystery of our redemption is enacted.

And so, Lord God, with angels and all saints
we exult and glorify your holy name:

Holy . . .

Holy Week – Wednesday

When terms such as 'majesty' or 'judgement' are used of God,
they have to be spoken, as it were, through the language of the
Passion of Jesus. This preface reflects on the mystery by which
the Cross of Christ reveals the reality of the God of Jesus. It is
also found in the Roman Sacramentary as the first preface of the
Passion.

It is truly right and just, our duty and our salvation,
always, here and everywhere to give you thanks,
Lord, holy Father, almighty and eternal God.

Through the saving passion of your Son
the whole world has been called
to acknowledge and to praise your majesty;
for in the wondrous power of the Cross
your judgement of this world is revealed
and the power of Christ the crucified shines forth.

And so, Lord God, with angels and all saints
we exult and glorify your holy name:

Holy . . .

Holy Week – Thursday, the Mass of Chrism

This preface celebrates the ministerial priesthood of the Church
as a gift of Christ, a sharing in his High Priesthood and a service
to Christ's people. Though the Chrism Mass has a wider field of
vision than simply the ordained priesthood, since the Chrism and
other oils are part of the Church's whole sacramental ministry,
yet it is through his priests that Christ celebrates these sacraments.
This preface is almost identical with that in the Roman Missal
for the Chrism Mass.

It is truly right and just, our duty and our salvation,
always, here and everywhere to give you thanks,
Lord, holy Father, almighty and eternal God.

By the anointing of the Holy Spirit you consecrated your
   only Son
High Priest of the new and eternal Covenant;
and in your mysterious purpose you ordain
that Christ's one priesthood shall continue in your Church.
Christ confers the dignity of royal priesthood
upon the people he has gained for you.
With love he chooses men
to share in his sacred ministry by the laying on of hands.
In his name, they will set forth before you
the sacrifice that has redeemed the human race
and spread the paschal banquet for your children.
They will serve the needs of your people with love,
feeding and refreshing them by word and sacraments.
They will offer their life in service to you
and for the salvation of their brothers and sisters.
They will strive to be formed in the likeness of Christ
as constant witnesses to you in faith and love.

And so, Lord God, with angels and all saints
we exult and glorify your holy name:

Holy . . .

Holy Week – Thursday, the Vespers Mass of the Lord's Supper

In the Ambrosian tradition this Mass is celebrated within the Liturgy of Evening Prayer. Though sharing many texts with the Roman Lord's Supper Mass, it has a different feel to it. There is no Washing of Feet and the 'tone' is that of a passiontide liturgy rather than a commemoration of the eucharist. Accordingly, the tone of this preface with its antitheses of freedom and binding, judge and judged, looks forward to the events of Good Friday.

It is truly right and just, our duty and our salvation,
always, here and everywhere to give you thanks,
Lord, holy Father, almighty and eternal God,
through Jesus Christ our Lord.

Though he was God most high,
he descended upon earth to blot out our sins;
though coming to set us free
our Lord was bound as a criminal
and sold for money by a slave.
Though judge of heaven's angels,
he was arraigned before a human judge
to free the human race, his own creation,
from the power of death.

Therefore with angels and saints
we sing the unceasing hymn of your glory:

Holy . . .

THE SEASON OF EASTER

Eastertime begins in the Ambrosian Rite with the great Vigil of Pascha, similar to that in the Roman Liturgy, though with slight differences in the choice of readings (for instance, Exodus 12:1–11 is used here and not on Holy Thursday evening).

The season of Easter lasts for fifty days, a chain of sacred numbers: seven weeks of seven days each plus one great day, the Solemnity of Pentecost. The entire time is described as being 'like one great Sunday' as the Missal states in its Introduction to the Calendar.

A cycle of prefaces is provided for Eastertime, which is repeated twice during the great fifty days.

The Vigil of Pascha

The Ambrosian Paschal Vigil uses the Preface of the Lamb, which is found in the Roman Rite too as Easter Preface I. In the light of the Vigil readings this preface connects with the story of Abraham's sacrifice and the injunctions concerning the Passover Lamb from Exodus 12. The sense is similar to that in the preface for the second Sunday after Christmas, that Christ is the summation of all that was foreshadowed in the Old Testament traditions of sacrifice.

It is truly right and just, our duty and our salvation,
to sing your praise, Lord God, in every season;
but most of all we are to praise you with exultant heart
on this most holy night
when Christ, our Passover, is sacrificed.

He is the true Lamb
who took away the sins of the world;
who by dying has destroyed our death
and by rising has restored our life.

And so, in the joy of this Passover
earth and heaven resound with gladness.
The angels and the powers of all creation
sing the ageless hymn of your glory:

Holy . . .

Easter Day

This highly coloured thanksgiving is a masterpiece. It celebrates the Paschal Mystery of Christ not simply in terms of the dying and rising but the whole sweep of foreshadowing and fulfilment. A source of inspiration is the Exsultet *from the Easter Vigil, now echoing once more on Easter morning.*

It is truly right and just, our duty and our salvation,
to give you thanks and praise, all-powerful God,
the uncreated Father, source and maker of all that is.

Your Son Jesus Christ, though one with you in glory,
accepted death on a cross for our salvation.
This is the Passover foreshadowed long ago
in the sacrifice of Isaac, Abraham's beloved son,
and prefigured in the offering of a lamb without blemish
according to the tradition of Moses.
This is the Passover of Christ,
acclaimed by prophets as the One who was to bear the sin
    of all
and blot out their iniquity.
This day is our Passover feast,
resplendent in the blood of Christ,
a day of rejoicing and gladness for all your faithful people.
O gracious gift ! O gift beyond all telling !
The feast to be honoured above all other feasts,
since on this day our Saviour Jesus Christ
brought us to freedom by freely giving his life.
O death most truly blessed, which burst the bonds of death
and vanquished the prince of darkness;
which drew us up from the depths of our fall
and raised us joyfully to heaven !

And so, with angels and archangels
and with all the powers of heaven,
we glorify your holy name
in this, their ageless hymn of praise:

Holy . . .

Easter Day – for the Baptized

The first Easter Day preface is lengthy, luxuriant and full of the theology of the Mystery. The second is different. With a simple clarity it sums up the heart of Easter as seen through the eyes of those who have been through it for the first time. Each day in Easter week the Ambrosian Rite has two masses, one of the day and a second for the new Christians baptized at the Vigil. We might think of them as people who perhaps for many years have known the mystery of God's gracious calling and the struggle to respond. Perhaps it was like it had been for Saint Augustine, himself baptized in Milan by Saint Ambrose: it came suddenly and simply. Here is something echoing Saint Peter's words: 'Like newborn infants, thirst for the pure spiritual milk' (cf. 1 Peter 2:2). Here is Easter seen with all the innocence of the newborn.

It is truly right and just, our duty and our salvation,
always, here and everywhere to give you thanks,
Lord, holy Father, almighty and eternal God.

Because the world of the past has gone
and fullness of life is restored to us in Christ.

And so, in the joy of this Passover,
earth and heaven resound with gladness;
the angels and the powers of all creation
sing the ageless hymn of your glory:

Holy . . .

Easter Monday

Eight days of intense rejoicing mark Easter week. The Baptized are prominent in the Church, they are the principal objects of its prayer. For those baptized some time ago, the yearly remembrance of their own liberation is joined to that of the universal reconciliation accomplished in Christ.

It is truly right and just, our duty and our salvation,
always, here and everywhere to give you thanks,
Lord, holy Father, almighty and eternal God.

As the days of this solemn feast return,
you call your people to celebrate more faithfully
the saving mystery of Christ's passion and resurrection;
so that what he has accomplished
in reconciling the world to you
may be celebrated with ever greater happiness.

And so, in the joy of this Passover,
earth and heaven resound with gladness.
The angels and the powers of all creation
sing the ageless hymn of your glory:

Holy . . .

Easter Monday – for the Baptized

Each day of Easter week is 'The Day'. For the Baptized, there
exists in these days of their first Easter a sense of newness. So
they will hear the words of this preface about Christ the firstfruits
with added keenness. They have received in their very body,
through the water and Chrism, the new robes and the light, the
promise of the glory of all flesh.

It is truly right and just, our duty and our salvation,
always, here and everywhere to give you thanks,
Lord, holy Father, almighty and eternal God.

We praise you with overflowing joy today
for the wonderful redemption of the human race.
This day shines out above all other days
for the dying and blessed rising of Christ our Lord.
This is the day when your eternal Son,
having power to lay down his life
and power to take it up again,
arose as firstborn from among the dead
to glorify our flesh and spirit,
that human nature which he had united to himself.

And so, in the joy of this Passover,
earth and heaven resound with gladness.
The angels and the powers of all creation
sing the ageless hymn of your glory:

Holy . . .

Easter Tuesday

Here is a preface that synthesizes what Easter is, a Passover of birth into eternal life, and even here in this age, a cause for anticipating the joy of the age to come.

Father most holy,
it is truly right to give you thanks,
it is right to give you glory
and to praise you in every season;
but most of all
in these recurring days of our salvation.

Through the paschal mystery of Christ
humanity comes to resurrection,
eternal life begins,
the source of enduring happiness is opened for us all.

And so, in the joy of this Passover,
earth and heaven resound with gladness.
The angels and the powers of all creation
sing the ageless hymn of your glory:

Holy . . .

Easter Tuesday – for the Baptized

*Some of the themes of Easter Baptism ring through this text,
particularly the echoes of Psalm 114: 'When Israel came out of
Egypt'.*

It is truly right and just, our duty and our salvation,
that we should give you glory, Lord, at all times
and praise you most joyfully on this day
when we celebrate the resurrection of our Lord Jesus Christ.

Today, when Christ arose from death,
the proud empire of Satan fell,
the gates of the dead were broken down,
the sentence due for our sins was revoked
and the terror of death brought to nothing.
Now indeed through spiritual waters, from slavery to
    freedom,
as it were from the dominion of Egypt,
Christ has led us in the triumph of his rising to glory.

And so, in the joy of this Passover,
earth and heaven resound with gladness.
The angels and the powers of all creation
sing the ageless hymn of your glory:

Holy . . .

Easter Wednesday

The paschal image of Christ as High Priest, developed in the Letter to the Hebrews, forms a significant part of the Easter preface themes.

It is truly right and just, our duty and our salvation,
to give you thanks, almighty Father, here and in every place,
because the day of our resurrection has dawned
in the transcendent glory of our Lord Jesus Christ.

Christ is the sacrifice, Christ the priest
who consecrates a people to you
by the shedding of his own blood
and presents them eternally
before the face of your glory.

And so, in the joy of this Passover,
earth and heaven resound with gladness.
The angels and the powers of all creation
sing the ageless hymn of your glory:

Holy . . .

Easter Wednesday – for the Baptized

Just as during Lent the prefaces looked back to Adam's fall and its undoing through Christ's lenten discipline, so again that theme is taken up in this preface. Easter is a renewal of humanity as God intended it to be.

It is truly right and just, our duty and our salvation,
always, here and everywhere to give you thanks,
Lord, holy Father, almighty and eternal God.

We celebrate with joy the feast of our redemption,
when human nature, freed from the bonds of ancient guilt,
enters into the new and living hope
of resurrection with Christ
and finds once more
the beauty and goodness of its first beginning.

And so, in the joy of this Passover,
earth and heaven resound with gladness.
The angels and the powers of all creation
sing the ageless hymn of your glory:

Holy . . .

Easter Thursday

This preface is similar to that in the Roman Missal of Easter V.
Once more appears the theme of Christ the priest of a new
sacrifice superseding all the sacrifices of old.

It is truly right and just, our duty and our salvation,
always, here and everywhere to give you thanks,
Lord, holy Father, almighty and eternal God,
through Jesus Christ our Lord.

By giving himself for our redemption,
Christ abolished the sacrifices of old
and he who is at once both priest and lamb
offered his body as the perfect sacrifice.

And so, in the joy of this Passover,
earth and heaven resound with gladness.
The angels and the powers of all creation
sing the ageless hymn of your glory:

Holy . . .

Easter Thursday – for the Baptized

For the newly Baptized, there awaited the eucharistic table where for the first time they fed upon that sacrifice in which they had been washed and anointed. Recalling that event, this preface speaks of that gift as the way to heaven.

It is truly right and just, our duty and our salvation,
always, here and everywhere to give you thanks,
Lord, holy Father, almighty and eternal God,
through Jesus Christ our Lord.

He gave himself in sacrifice for us,
so that by his body and blood
which sets us free from all sin,
we might be nourished in a heavenly sacrifice unto eternal
   life.

And so, in the joy of this Passover,
earth and heaven resound with gladness.
The angels and the powers of all creation
sing the ageless hymn of your glory:

Holy . . .

Easter Friday

*Easter throws wide the gates of heaven for the Passover pilgrimage
to enter in. This preface is also found in the Roman Sacramentary
as the Preface of Easter II.*

It is truly right and just, our duty and our salvation,
to praise you, Lord, at all times
and now to glorify you with greater acclaim;
for Christ, our Passover, is sacrificed.

Through Christ the children of light rise to eternal life,
and the gate of heaven's kingdom is opened to his people.
For by his death we are redeemed from death
and in his rising, life springs up for all.

And so, in the joy of this Passover,
earth and heaven resound with gladness.
The angels and the powers of all creation
sing the ageless hymn of your glory:

Holy . . .

Easter Friday – for the Baptized

'From the depth of our fall', as the Easter Day preface put it,
God drew forth resurrection. So this preface expands on that idea
in a series of antitheses, culminating in lines derived from Saint
Paul (cf. the reiteration of 'one' in Romans 5:16,17,18).

It is truly right and just, our duty and our salvation,
always, here and everywhere to give you thanks,
Lord, holy Father, almighty and eternal God,
through Jesus Christ our Lord.

From his death, life has arisen;
from the passion, salvation comes forth.
The agony of the cross yields the remedy of love,
condemnation is turned to triumph,
and wounds are for our healing.
For the one man, Jesus Christ,
chose to suffer death
so that all might be made alive for ever.

And so, in the joy of this Passover,
earth and heaven resound with gladness.
The angels and the powers of all creation
sing the ageless hymn of your glory:

Holy . . .

Easter Saturday

On the last day of the Easter week, the preface speaks of the 'day of our salvation' inasmuch as every day of this week is Easter, to be solemnized with the Easter sacrament of the eucharist.

It is truly right and just, our duty and our salvation,
always, here and everywhere to give you thanks,
Lord, holy Father, almighty and eternal God.

We rejoice above all at this time
to celebrate in a solemn observance
the day that brought us salvation
and the wonderful mystery of your compassion towards us.
For by this mystery we are delivered
from the darkness of our ancient captivity,
to become children of light and liberty;
and, freed now from the bonds of earth
we pass over into the kingdom of heaven.

And so, in the joy of this Passover,
earth and heaven resound with gladness.
The angels and the powers of all creation
sing the ageless hymn of your glory:

Holy . . .

Easter Saturday – for the Baptized

The Letter to the Hebrews again forms the foundation for this preface, as Christ is acclaimed as the High Priest and Lamb.

It is truly right and just, our duty and our salvation,
always, here and everywhere to give you thanks,
Lord, holy Father, almighty and eternal God,
through Jesus Christ our Lord.

Faithful is his promise
and unchanging is his truth;
for he stands as our high priest for ever,
of all priests the only one who has no need
for the forgiveness of sins.
Indeed, he is himself the true Lamb
who washed away the sin of the world.

And so, in the joy of this Passover,
earth and heaven resound with gladness.
The angels and the powers of all creation
sing the ageless hymn of your glory:

Holy . . .

Sunday 2 of Easter

The preface for this Sunday takes words from Saint Paul's baptismal treatise in the Letter to the Romans about walking 'in newness of life' (cf. Romans 6:4).

It is truly right and just, our duty and our salvation,
always, here and everywhere to give you thanks,
Lord, holy Father, almighty and eternal God,
through Jesus Christ our Lord.

Through his Passover from death to life
Christ has taught us to leave our former self behind
and to walk in newness of spirit.
By him the bitterness of death is overcome
and the fullness of life eternal
is bestowed upon his people.

And so, in the joy of this Passover,
earth and heaven resound with gladness.
The angels and the powers of all creation
sing the ageless hymn of your glory:

Holy . . .

Monday 2 of Easter

The opening lines of this preface recall those in the Roman Sacramentary for Sundays of the Year V. The ancient Ambrosian source, however, includes these lines as the preliminary to an Easter preface. That source has been fully retained for this Sunday.

It is truly right and just, our duty and our salvation,
always, here and everywhere to give you thanks,
Lord, holy Father, almighty and eternal God.

You are the maker of all things,
you have decreed the changing of times and seasons;
to man and woman, formed in wisdom as your likeness,
you have given the care of this wonderful creation
and all that lives within its bounds.
Though we are creatures of earth,
you give the life of heaven in the new birth of baptism.
For you have conquered the power of death
and bestowed on us the gift of immortality,
and when we had lost our way through sinfulness
you have brought us back to the path of truth.

Therefore with angels and saints
we sing the unceasing hymn of your glory:

Holy . . .

Wednesday 2 of Easter

The Tuesday preface is the same as that for the Second Sunday.
This Wednesday preface takes up the theme of the Paschal Mys-
tery as a restoration of the divine likeness in human nature.

It is truly right and just, our duty and our salvation,
to give thanks to you, the all-powerful Father
and in these days of Easter
to celebrate with sincere and joyful heart
the memory of your wonderful works.

Christ Jesus, your only Son,
has conquered the powers of the world and of evil
by the wonderful mystery of his passion,
restoring your likeness in man and woman,
to place them once more in paradise
and open to them the gate of life eternal.

And so, in the joy of this Passover,
earth and heaven resound with gladness.
The angels and the powers of all creation
sing the ageless hymn of your glory:

Holy . . .

Thursday 2 of Easter

The theme of restoration is once again taken up in this preface,
which looks forward to the glorification of our flesh through the
rising of Jesus.

It is truly right and just, our duty and our salvation,
always, here and everywhere to give you thanks,
Lord, holy Father, almighty and eternal God,
through Jesus Christ our Lord.

By his blood he has ransomed us from slavery,
so that our human nature
which in Adam became subject to death
might be recalled to its eternal destiny
in the glory of heaven.

And so, with all the choirs of angels,
we praise your glory, now and for ever
as with one voice we sing:

Holy . . .

Friday 2 of Easter

The way of Christ is a way of descent and ascent: into death and from there into life. It is the way of the Baptized as they enter and leave the saving waters, following in the Lord's footsteps.

It is truly right and just, our duty and our salvation,
always, here and everywhere to give you thanks,
Lord, holy Father, almighty and eternal God,
through Jesus Christ our Lord.

In Adam's fall, the human race knew death;
now through the suffering of Christ it is made new.
For Christ has followed our human journey
even into the harshness of death,
so that he might call us to follow his footsteps
through the resurrection into eternal life.

And so, in the joy of this Passover,
earth and heaven resound with gladness.
The angels and the powers of all creation
sing the ageless hymn of your glory:

Holy . . .

Saturday 2 of Easter

A short text, dwelling on the fulfilment of the Covenant in the blood of Christ.

It is truly right and just, our duty and our salvation,
always, here and everywhere to give you thanks,
Lord, holy Father, almighty and eternal God,
through Jesus Christ our Lord.

By his death, and through the shedding of his blood
Christ brought to completion the Covenant of old
and made us heirs with himself
to his heavenly and eternal life.

And so, in the joy of this Passover
earth and heaven resound with gladness.
The angels and the powers of all creation
sing the ageless hymn of your glory:

Holy . . .

Friday 3 of Easter

The prefaces for Easter, week 3 are repeated from earlier in the season as follows: Monday = Monday of Easter Week; Tuesday = Saturday of Easter Week; Wednesday = Wednesday of Easter Week; Thursday = Sunday 2 of Easter. This Friday preface is found also in the Roman Sacramentary where it is the Preface of Sundays of the Year II.

It is truly right and just, our duty and our salvation,
always, here and everywhere to give you thanks,
Lord, holy Father, almighty and eternal God,
through Jesus Christ our Lord.

In compassion for us who were sinners,
he humbled himself to be born of the Virgin;
through suffering and through dying
he delivered us from unending death
and by his rising, he gave us eternal life.

And so, with all the choirs of angels,
we praise your glory, now and for ever
as with one voice we sing:

Holy . . .

Saturday 3 of Easter

This preface, found three times in the Ambrosian Easter series, is a concise summation of the high priestly theme. It is found also in the Roman Sacramentary as Easter Preface III.

It is truly right and just, our duty and our salvation,
to praise you, Lord, at all times,
and now to glorify you with greater acclaim
for Christ, our Passover, is sacrificed.

He continues to offer himself for us,
to plead our cause eternally before you;
Christ is the sacrifice who dies no more,
Christ has been slain, and now is alive for ever.

And so, in the joy of this Passover,
earth and heaven resound with gladness.
The angels and the powers of all creation
sing the ageless hymn of your glory:

Holy . . .

Sunday 5 of Easter

The prefaces for week 4 of Easter are repeated from those of week 2, except for that of the Sunday, which is from Friday of week 3, and Tuesday, which is from Sunday 2. This preface for Sunday 5 speaks of the unity of believers with the glorified Christ.

It is truly right and just, our duty and our salvation,
always, here and everywhere to give you thanks, Lord God,
but most of all in this holy Easter season.
Now, in faith and reverence
your Church celebrates the paschal mystery of Christ;
so that the body of those who believe
may be made one with his sufferings
and one with his resurrection to eternal life.

And so, in the joy of this Passover,
earth and heaven resound with gladness.
The angels and the powers of all creation
sing the ageless hymn of your glory:

Holy . . .

Weeks Five, Six and Seven of Easter

For the fifth and sixth weeks of Easter the prefaces are repeated as follows: Monday 5 = Monday of Easter Week; Tuesday = Saturday of Easter Week; Wednesday = Wednesday of Easter Week; Thursday = Sunday 2 of Easter; Friday = Friday of week 3; Saturday = Saturday of week 3; Sunday 6 of Easter = Saturday of week 3; Monday 6 = Monday of week 2; Tuesday = Sunday 2 of Easter; Wednesday, morning Mass = Wednesday of week 2.

The prefaces for Ascension Vigil and Day are given below.

The preface for Friday of week 6 is a repeat of that for Friday of week 2; Saturday = Saturday of week 2.

The Preface for Sunday 7 of Easter is printed below.

The prefaces for the days between Ascension and Pentecost are arranged as follows: Sunday 7 of Easter – printed below; Monday 7 – printed below; Tuesday 7 – printed below; Wednesday 7 – printed below; Thursday 7 = Preface of the Vigil of Ascension Day; Friday 7 – printed below.

The Pentecost prefaces (Vigil and Day and 'for the Baptized') are printed below.

The Vigil of the Ascension (Wednesday 6, Evening Mass)

Christ's glorified body shares in the flesh of Adam, so that what had fallen prey to the devil is now glorified in Christ. The ancient Ambrosian source for this preface also provided material to the revised Roman Missal, for its Preface 1 of Advent.

It is truly right and just, our duty and our salvation,
always, here and everywhere to give you thanks,
Lord, holy Father, almighty and eternal God.

We praise you above all on this day
when Jesus Christ your Son our Lord
brought to completion the mystery of our salvation
and fulfilled the plan you formed long ago;
that in his human body
he should conquer and humble the devil,
the enemy of your divine work,
and lead our mortal nature to share the life of heaven.

And so, in the joy of this Passover,
earth and heaven resound with gladness.
The angels and the powers of all creation
sing the ageless hymn of your glory:

Holy . . .

Ascension Day

This preface dwells on the significance of Christ both as Mediator (cf. 1 Timothy 2:5) and as firstfruits (cf. Colossians 1:18). His Ascension is a source of hope, as he is the head, always united to his body (cf. Ephesians 5:23). This preface is also found in the Roman Missal for Ascension Day.

It is truly right and just, our duty and our salvation,
always, here and everywhere to give you thanks,
Lord, holy Father, almighty and eternal God:

Because the Lord Jesus, the King of glory,
triumphant over sin and death,
has ascended to the highest heaven
as the angels looked on in wonder.
Christ, the Mediator between God and humankind,
Judge of the world and Lord of the heavenly powers,
has not forsaken our human lowliness,
but has given us the hope
that we, his members, might follow him to heaven,
where he, our head and our beginning, has gone before us.

And so, in the joy of this Passover,
earth and heaven resound with gladness.
The angels and the powers of all creation
sing the ageless hymn of your glory:

Holy . . .

Sunday 7 of Easter

In the light of the Ascension hope that Christ's members will follow him to heaven, the preface for the Sunday after Ascension sees the whole of the Mystery of Christ as a cause of our salvation.

It is truly right and just, our duty and our salvation,
always, here and everywhere to give you thanks,
Lord, holy Father, almighty and eternal God;
through Jesus Christ our Lord:

Who by his birth came to the rescue of humankind,
and by suffering our death, has overcome the world;
who in the glory of the resurrection
opened the way to life eternal
and by his ascension, gave us the hope
of ascending into heaven.

And so, in the joy of this Passover,
earth and heaven resound with gladness.
The angels and the powers of all creation
sing the ageless hymn of your glory:

Holy . . .

Monday 7 of Easter

The promise made by Christ was to send the Holy Spirit upon the disciples (cf. John 14:16, 26). Accordingly, the time between Ascension and Pentecost is a time of expectation. This preface narrates the sequence. A slightly less elaborate form of this text is found in the Roman Missal as the Preface of the Holy Spirit, I.

It is truly right and just, our duty and our salvation,
always, here and everywhere to give you thanks,
Lord, holy Father, almighty and eternal God;
through Jesus Christ our Lord.

Ascending in glory above the highest heaven,
seated at your right hand in power and majesty,
he poured out the promised Holy Spirit
upon your adopted children.

And so, with all the choirs of angels,
we praise your glory, now and for ever
as with one voice we sing:

Holy . . .

Wednesday 7 of Easter

Ancient Christianity pulled no punches in its confident assertions about salvation and the purposes of God for a redeemed humanity. The Fathers took the bold statements of Saint Peter and Saint Paul about sharing the nature of God (cf. for instance Ephesians 2:4–6 and 1 Peter 1:3–4) as a source for their eucharistic thanksgivings. This preface, found also in the Roman Sacramentary as the Preface of Ascension II, is typical of this boldness.

It is truly right and just, our duty and our salvation,
always, here and everywhere to give you thanks,
Lord, holy Father, almighty and eternal God;
through Jesus Christ our Lord:

Who after his rising from the dead
showed himself plainly to his disciples,
and in their sight was taken up into heaven
that he might make us partakers of his divinity.

And so, in the joy of this Passover,
earth and heaven resound with gladness.
The angels and the powers of all creation
sing the ageless hymn of your glory:

Holy . . .

Friday 7 of Easter

To share in Christ's divine life represents the goal not just of the New Testament, but also of the Old, for it had promised the Spirit of God as the gift of the end time (cf. Joel 2:28 quoted by Saint Peter on Pentecost Day, cf. Acts 2:17).

It is truly right and just, our duty and our salvation,
always, here and everywhere to give you thanks,
Lord, holy Father, almighty and eternal God;

Christ, the true Lamb, his passion accomplished,
has ascended to your right hand,
so that by the outpouring of the Holy Spirit
upon the apostles and upon those who believe,
he might show the fulfilment of the gifts
promised in the Law of old,
and reveal the making of the new Covenant.

And so, in the joy of this Passover,
earth and heaven resound with gladness.
The angels and the powers of all creation
sing the ageless hymn of your glory:

Holy . . .

Saturday 7 of Easter

On the morning before Pentecost, an eschatological aspect of the coming feast is highlighted in the preface. The Christ who bestows the Holy Spirit is the One who is to come to do justice for the living and the dead.

It is truly right and just, our duty and our salvation,
always, here and everywhere to give you thanks,
Lord, holy Father, almighty and eternal God,
through Jesus Christ our Lord.

He humbled himself
to accomplish the mystery of our salvation
and now, enthroned at your right hand in glory,
he bears our mortal nature united to himself;
thus to bestow upon the Church his Holy Spirit,
thus to return as Judge of the living and the dead.

And so, with all the choirs of angels,
we praise your glory, now and for ever,
as with one voice we sing:

Holy . . .

The Vigil Mass of Pentecost

The opening lines of this preface (reminiscent of the Roman Pentecost Day preface) look forward to the feast as the fulfilment of the 'Great Fifty Days' of Easter. With distinctively Christian hopefulness, the last half of the preface looks beyond the day itself to the glory that is already begun for believers by virtue of their union, here and now, with Christ.

It is truly right and just, our duty and our salvation,
always, here and everywhere to give you thanks,
Lord, holy Father, almighty and eternal God.

Today you bestowed the gifts of the Holy Spirit
on your adopted sons and daughters,
those you had called into fellowship with your Son;
and so you brought the paschal mystery to its fulfilment.
You give the firstfruits of an eternal inheritance
to all whom you have made co-heirs with Christ,
so that, redeemed by him and enriched by the Spirit,
they may live in the sure and certain hope
of coming to share his eternal glory.

And so, in the joy of this Passover,
earth and heaven resound with gladness.
The angels and the powers of all creation
sing the ageless hymn of your glory:

Holy . . .

Pentecost Day

*One of the themes of Christian preaching in the time of the
evolution of the western liturgies was that the gift of tongues on
Pentecost Day had put to rights the 'confusion of languages'
visited upon humankind in the story of the Tower of Babel (cf.
Genesis 11). The Babel narrative, in other words, served Pentecost
preachers as a sort of 'Fall' image, to be reversed by the unity of
one faith-confession found in the gift of the Spirit. The use of
the Babel myth as an antithetical image for Pentecost is the main
theme of this preface.*

It is truly right and just, our duty and our salvation,
to celebrate the joy of this most holy day,
which in its sacred numbering of fifty days
enacts the fullness of the paschal mystery.

Today the confusion of languages
which human pride had brought upon the world
is resolved by the gift of the Holy Spirit.
Today, hearing the sound come suddenly from heaven,
the apostles received the profession of one faith
and spoke in many tongues,
announcing the glory of your Gospel
to all the nations of the earth.

And so, in the joy of this Passover,
earth and heaven resound with gladness.
The angels and the powers of all creation
sing the ageless hymn of your glory:

Holy . . .

Pentecost Day – for the Baptized

As with Easter and the week following it, there is today a special Mass formulary for those who have been baptized. Strangely, this contains no explicit mention of Pentecost. It is simply a piece of picture language, telling of our ascension to heaven through the descent of Christ.

It is truly right and just, our duty and our salvation,
always, here and everywhere to give you thanks,
Lord, holy Father, almighty and eternal God,
through Jesus Christ our Lord.

In compassion beyond words
he came down to our lowliness,
that he might raise us up in his surpassing splendour,
and from our fallen earthly state
he has exalted us to the glory of heaven.

And so, with angels and archangels
and with all the powers of heaven,
we glorify your holy name
in this, their ageless hymn of praise:

Holy . . .

Pentecost Day – for the Baptized

A second Pentecost Mass is given in the Ambrosian Missal for the Baptized. The preface of this Mass is explicitly about the Spirit, the gifts it gives to the Church and the unity it creates. A similar preface is found in the Roman Missal 'For Christian Unity'.

It is truly right and just, our duty and our salvation,
always, here and everywhere to give you thanks,
Lord, holy Father, almighty and eternal God,
as we celebrate today the coming of the Holy Spirit.

In the first days of the Church
your Spirit imparted to all peoples
both knowledge of your Godhead
and the power of speech to tell of your wonders.
Through many gifts that differ
the Spirit works a wonderful unity;
in the variety of what is bestowed
the Spirit imparts all things in wisdom;
indeed, it is the selfsame Spirit
who creates the many tongues that proclaim your word
and yet bestows the faith that brings them into one.

And so, in the joy of this Passover,
earth and heaven resound with gladness.
The angels and the powers of all creation
sing the ageless hymn of your glory:

Holy . . .

ORDINARY TIME

The Ambrosian Rite has thirty-two weeks of 'Ordinary Time' as it is known. But no time is ordinary in the economy of Christ's Incarnation. 'All time is Christ's, and all the ages', we say in the Easter Vigil. The title 'Ordinary Time' refers to those weeks not part of either the Christmas Cycle or that of Lent/Easter. The Ambrosian Sacramentary describes these weeks as a time when 'the whole mystery of Christ is recalled in its fullness, especially on Sundays' (Universal Norms for the Liturgical Year no. 42).

Ordinary Time Feasts

Some important feasts are celebrated during Ordinary Time: the Holy Family on the fourth Sunday of January; the Holy Trinity on the Sunday after Pentecost; the Body and Blood of Christ on the Thursday after Trinity Sunday; the Sacred Heart on the Friday after the Second Sunday after Pentecost; the Dedication of the Cathedral on the third Sunday of October; Christ the King on the last Sunday of Ordinary Time.

The prefaces for these days, with the exception of the Holy Family, are the same as those in the Roman Sacramentary. The Holy Family Preface is unique to the Ambrosian Liturgy.

The Holy Family of Jesus, Mary and Joseph

This preface locates the Holy Family within the context of the Mystery of Salvation and offers it as a model for the values of family life.

It is truly right and just, our duty and our salvation,
always, here and everywhere to give you thanks,
Lord, holy Father, almighty and eternal God,
through Jesus Christ our Lord.

Proceeding from your very heart,
yet in your wonderful purpose becoming one like us,
Christ made himself part of a human family
as a witness to the order of nature,
and a restoration by grace of the human family
to its original dignity.
In that household there flourished chastity in marriage;
there the Son of God was subject to an earthly father
and there sweet peace engendered a fellowship of love.
That humble house of David's line was blessed and holy,
and there the mystery of our redemption
was sheltered at its first beginnings.

And so, with angels and archangels
and with all the powers of heaven,
we glorify your holy name
in this, their ageless hymn of praise:

Holy . . .

The Holy Trinity

This early medieval piece, so carefully phrased, is common to both the Ambrosian and the Roman Liturgy.

It is truly right and just, our duty and our salvation,
always, here and everywhere to give you thanks,
Lord, holy Father, almighty and eternal God:

Who with your only Son and the Holy Spirit
are one God and one Lord:
not in the unity of one single person
but in a Threefold yet single being;
and that which by your revelation
we believe as touching your glory,
that too we believe without distinction
of your Son and of the Holy Spirit.
In professing your true and eternal Godhead
three distinct persons we adore,
though one in being and equal in majesty.

Earth and heaven praise you,
angels and archangels worship you
and all the saints acclaim you, saying:

Holy . . .

The Body and Blood of Christ

The Ambrosian Sacramentary gives two prefaces for this feast.
The first preface was created for the Roman Missal of 1969. It
combines both the theological themes of Christ's self offering for
the unity of the human race and some more traditional
'devotional' language about the fruits of receiving the sacrament.

It is truly right and just, our duty and our salvation,
always, here and everywhere to give you thanks,
Lord, holy Father, almighty and eternal God,
through Jesus Christ our Lord.

As he ate with his apostles at the Last Supper,
Christ offered himself to you as the Lamb without blemish,
the acceptable sacrifice of perfect praise.
He willed to continue throughout the ages
the memorial of his saving cross.
In this holy sacrament
you feed and sanctify your people,
so that the human race that shares one earth
may be enlightened by one faith
and joined together in one bond of love.
To your table and to this great sacrament we come,
to be enfolded in the sweetness of your gift
and transformed into the likeness of heaven.

And so, with all the choirs of angels,
we praise your glory, now and for ever,
as with one voice we sing:

Holy . . .

The Body and Blood of Christ

*Using a form of words common in ancient French and Spanish
eucharistic prayers, this preface looks to Christ as at one and the
same time the saving sacrifice and its perpetuation in the offering
of the eucharist. One sacrifice, one priest: these early prayers saw
no distinction between the two offerings.*

It is truly right and just, our duty and our salvation,
always, here and everywhere to give you thanks,
Lord, holy Father, almighty and eternal God,
through Jesus Christ our Lord.

He is the true and everlasting priest
who established for us the form of the eternal sacrifice;
he offered himself to you as a victim for our salvation
and taught us to offer that same sacrifice as his memorial.
When we eat the body sacrificed for us
we are made strong
and when we drink the blood shed for us
we are washed clean.

And so, with angels and archangels
and with all the powers of heaven,
we glorify your holy name
in this, their ageless hymn of praise:

Holy . . .

The Sacred Heart of Jesus

Though this feast probably originated in late medieval devotion to the Passion of Jesus, its status as a liturgical feast necessitates a preface that portrays the Heart of Jesus in a way related to liturgical worship. Accordingly, the scriptural image of the piercing of Jesus' side was chosen (cf. John 19:34). In the Fathers and in the teaching of the Second Vatican Council (cf. Constitution on the Liturgy Sacrosanctum Concilium n. 5) the blood and water were seen as the source of the Church's great Sacraments of Baptism and Eucharist.

It is truly right and just, our duty and our salvation,
always, here and everywhere to give you thanks,
Lord, holy Father, almighty and eternal God,
through Jesus Christ our Lord.

He gave himself for us in wondrous love
and was lifted up on the cross;
then from his pierced side he poured out blood and water,
from which the Church's sacraments flow forth;
that all might be drawn to the Saviour's opened heart,
there to draw water joyfully from the fountain of salvation.

And so, with angels and archangels
and with all the powers of heaven,
we glorify your holy name
in this, their ageless hymn of praise:

Holy . . .

The Dedication of the Cathedral Church

To our anti-triumphalist age this preface will be hard to hear.
It is the product of a community that had not yet learned to
make a systematic distinction between Christ and the Church. It
is close in some ways to the Second Vatican Council's teaching,
when its Constitution on the Church speaks in the same scriptural
imagery. The Church has nothing it has not received from Christ.

It is truly right and just, our duty and our salvation,
always, here and everywhere to give you thanks,
Lord, holy Father, almighty and eternal God,
through Jesus Christ our Lord.

Christ has given to his Church
that same authority you gave to him,
and has established her as Bride and Queen.
To this authority he has committed all things
and what she binds on earth, he commands also in heaven.
The Church is Mother to all who live,
made glorious by the multitude of sons and daughters
whom day by day, through the Holy Spirit,
she bears as children of God.
She is the fruitful vine, whose branches fill the earth:
whose boughs, supported by the cross,
rise to the heights of the heavenly kingdom.
She is that city, built high on a hill,
clearly seen and visible to all,
which Christ your Son, our Lord, has founded
and in which he makes his dwelling.

And so, with angels and archangels
and with all the powers of heaven,
we glorify your holy name
in this, their ageless hymn of praise:

Holy . . .

Our Lord Jesus Christ, Universal King

This is the same preface, composed for the feast of Christ the King in the former Roman Missal, which appears in the revised Roman and Ambrosian Sacramentary.

It is truly right and just, our duty and our salvation,
always, here and everywhere to give you thanks,
Lord, holy Father, almighty and eternal God.

You anointed your only Son, our Lord Jesus Christ,
with the oil of gladness
as priest for ever and universal King,
so that, by offering himself on the altar of the cross
as the pure sacrifice that brings us peace,
he might accomplish the mystery of our redemption
and, having made all things subject to himself,
might present before your glory
an eternal and universal rule;
a rule of truth and life,
a rule of holiness and grace,
a rule of justice, love and peace.

And so, with angels and archangels
and with all the powers of heaven,
we glorify your holy name
in this, their ageless hymn of praise:

Holy . . .

ORDINARY TIME SUNDAYS

The Sunday prefaces of Ordinary Time will also be used during the following week when no feast occurs. In practice this will be less often, as many feasts in the Ambrosian Rite are assigned their own preface. In addition, the stock of common prefaces for saints' days is much larger than it is in the Roman Sacramentary. The Ambrosian Missal has no prefaces designated specifically for the weekdays of Ordinary Time.

The prefaces include the Roman Sunday prefaces, except for nos. 3 and 8. Many of the prefaces are used twice during the cycle.

Sunday 1

The Christmas feel of this preface is no accident, since the first few Sundays of Ordinary Time fall between Epiphany and Candlemas (2 February). Something of our own traditional prolongation of Christmas until the feast of the Presentation is evident in the Ambrosian Rite. The Latin is complex and this version is perhaps more of a paraphrase. I have substituted the term 'sin' for the Latin 'diabolus'.

It is truly right and just, our duty and our salvation,
always, here and everywhere to give you thanks,
Lord, holy Father, almighty and eternal God.

Through Christ, the fruit of the Virgin's womb,
you brought forgiveness to the human race,
condemned at its beginning through disobedience.
By your eternal Son you created all things;
now through his coming as God in human form
you have begun the new creation.
Where sin had triumphed over Adam
in the weakness of our mortal flesh,
your justice has prevailed and sin is overthrown
by your own Godhead in that same flesh incarnate.

And so, with angels and archangels
and with all the powers of heaven,
we glorify your holy name
in this, their ageless hymn of praise:

Holy . . .

Sunday 2

This thanksgiving is shot through with a joy that rests on confi-
dence in God's continuing blessings. These blessings both culmi-
nate in and are assured by the Incarnation of the Word.

It is truly right and just, our duty and our salvation,
always, here and everywhere to give you thanks,
Lord, holy Father, almighty and eternal God,
and with a voice of exultation
to sing the praises of your saving power.

You lift from us the weight of this life's troubles;
you console us with your many gifts;
but greatest of all is the joy of salvation
which you have bestowed upon us
by sending forth from the height of heaven
Christ the Lord as our Redeemer.

Through Christ the choirs of angels
worship forever with joy before your majesty;
with them, we pray you, join our voices
in this, their hymn of joyful supplication:

Holy . . .

Sunday 3

The Liturgy gives thanks for what has come to pass, but also expands awareness of God's present reality as our Saviour. Seen from the perspective of Ordinary Time, the Nativity of the Son of God is the first of God's saving acts in Christ.

It is truly right and just, our duty and our salvation,
always, here and everywhere to give you thanks,
Lord, holy Father, almighty and eternal God,
and in every season to offer you our praise.

In you we live and move and have our being;
no day, no moment leaves us
without the blessing of your constant love.
But most of all at this time
we should celebrate and acclaim you,
because the remembrance of the birth of Christ
has given us the sign that our redemption has begun;
and while we celebrate with new joy
the things that have come to pass,
we acknowledge also in these days
the gift of your abiding blessing.

And so, with all the choirs of angels,
we praise your glory, now and for ever
as with one voice we sing:

Holy . . .

Sunday 4 and 19

*God and humanity have exchanged their very selves. In Christ
God receives human nature. In Christ humanity receives a share
in the divine nature. Such an image of exchange is developed in
this preface. The celebration of the eucharist enacts a saving event.
The saving event becomes saving mystery in the Liturgy. The well
known Roman prayer might serve as a summary of this serene
preface: 'Whenever the memorial of this sacrifice is celebrated,
the work of our redemption is achieved.'*

It is truly right and just, our duty and our salvation,
always, here and everywhere to give you thanks,
Lord, holy Father, almighty and eternal God.

You give to the Church of Christ
his mysteries to celebrate,
by which you work a wonderful exchange:
for our mortal nature you give immortal life;
for our existence in a universe of time
you give an eternal destiny;
for our slavery to the power of death
you give the glory of resurrection.

And so, Lord God, with angels and all saints
we exult and glorify your holy name:

Holy . . .

Sunday 5 and 20

This is really a preface about Sunday, the Lord's day, a day typified by the Church's gathering for Word and Eucharist. The Italian version of this preface makes the sense plain by using the term 'Lord's Day' while giving the word 'Today' as its weekday alternative. This English version reflects the Italian translation.

It is truly right and just, our duty and our salvation,
always, here and everywhere to give you thanks,
Lord, holy Father, almighty and eternal God.

On this, the day of the Lord,*
you gather his people together
to celebrate his paschal mystery of redemption.
By your saving word you teach us,
and in the supper of the Lord
you feed this assembly with the bread of heaven;
so that with joy we may know ourselves
as a people reborn to a living hope,
and walking in the fellowship of love
as we await in faith the return of our Saviour.

Through Christ the choirs of angels
worship forever with joy before your majesty;
with them, we pray you, join our voices
in this, their hymn of joyful supplication:

Holy . . .

---

* *On weekdays is said:* Today you gather . . .

154

Sunday 6 and 21

This preface celebrates the offering of the eucharist and its goal.
The eucharist is the mystery of unity. However, such unity is no
human construction. The many are made one by the power of
the Holy Spirit who is invoked in the Mass to make the assembly
'... one body, one spirit in Christ' (cf. Eucharistic Prayer III in
the Roman and Ambrosian Missals).

It is truly right and just, our duty and our salvation,
always, here and everywhere to give you thanks,
Lord, holy Father, almighty and eternal God.

From your gift to us we offer you this sacrifice,
a holy and unfathomable mystery,
which, though offered by many to your glory,
is made the one body of Christ
by the inpouring of the Holy Spirit.
And we likewise, who share the communion
of this one bread and cup,
are united by faith as one body in Christ.

Through Christ the choirs of angels
worship forever with joy before your majesty;
with them, we pray you, join our voices
in this, their hymn of joyful supplication:

Holy ...

Sunday 7 and 22

Using ancient sources, this preface weaves together words largely from Saint Peter's First Letter, though also from Exodus and the Apocalypse (cf. Exodus 19:5,6; 1 Peter 2:9; Apocalypse 1:5,6 and 5:9,10), to celebrate the risen life of Christ in the Church, the 'people for your own possession'. This preface was created for the revised Roman Missal of 1969 and adopted by the Ambrosian Sacramentary. Echoes of the same themes may also be found in sources derived from the Sunday prefaces proposed in the Book of Common Prayer of 1927/8.

It is truly right and just, our duty and our salvation,
always, here and everywhere to give you thanks,
Lord, holy Father, almighty and eternal God,
through Jesus Christ our Lord.

By the mystery of his death and resurrection
Christ has accomplished a wonderful work.
From the yoke of slavery to sin and death
he has called us to share his glory
and receive the name of chosen race and royal priesthood,
holy nation and people for your own possession.
He bids us everywhere proclaim your mighty works
for you, our Father, have summoned us forth from darkness
into your own marvellous light.

Through Christ the choirs of angels
worship forever with joy before your majesty;
with them, we pray you, join our voices
in this, their hymn of joyful supplication:

Holy . . .

Sunday 8 and 23

This preface is an Easter preface. It is given for Friday 3, Sunday 4 and Friday 5 of Eastertide.

Sunday 9 and 24

This preface is the same as that in the Roman Missal, no. 4 of Sundays of Ordinary Time.

It is truly right and just, our duty and our salvation,
always, here and everywhere to give you thanks,
Lord, holy Father, almighty and eternal God,
through Jesus Christ our Lord.

By his birth, he renewed our former self;
by suffering death, he wiped away our sins.
By rising from the dead, he opened the way to eternal life
and by ascending to you, the Father,
he unlocked the gates of heaven.

Therefore with angels and saints
we sing the unceasing hymn of your glory:

Holy . . .

Sunday 10 and 25

Catholic and Orthodox Christian teaching understands the human race to have a responsibility to the world which God has created and of which it forms an inseparable part. This preface (also found in the Roman Missal for Sundays of Ordinary Time) images humanity as a priest, making eucharist before God for the wonders of his creation. In the theology of our day, the issue of how we relate to the world is a controversial one. The Latin original of this preface (though not its ancient sources) speaks of the 'lordship' of humanity over creation. Not surprisingly, modern versions are shy of this. The Italian adds the notion of human beings 'interpreting' God's purposes. English versions tend to omit the idea. This translation has partly followed the Italian example.

It is truly right and just, our duty and our salvation,
always, here and everywhere to give you thanks
Lord, holy Father, almighty and eternal God.

You are the maker of all things,
you have decreed the changing of times and seasons.
You fashioned the human race in your likeness
and entrusted to them the care of your wonderful works
that they might set forward your purpose for creation
and praise you for the wonderful work of your hands
through Jesus Christ our Lord.

Through Christ the choirs of angels
worship forever with joy before your majesty
with them, we pray you, join our voices
in this, their hymn of joyful supplication:

Holy . . .

Sunday 11 and 26

An earlier preface in this series (Ordinary Time Sunday 3) began with the same opening line, but whereas that text looked back to the 'Christmas feast' this one looks forward to the 'eternal Easter' whose promise we celebrate in every mass. This preface is also found in the Roman Missal where it is allotted as preface 6 for the Sundays of Ordinary Time.

It is truly right and just, our duty and our salvation,
always, here and everywhere to give you thanks,
Lord, holy Father, almighty and eternal God.

In you we live and move and have our being;
each day we encounter the signs of your tender care.
In the life of this mortal body
we receive even now the pledges of immortality.
Possessing the firstfruits of the Spirit
who raised Jesus from the dead,
we hope that the mystery of his dying and rising
will be for us also an eternal Easter.

And so, Lord God, with angels and all saints
we exult and glorify your holy name:

Holy . . .

Sunday 12 and 27

Christ stands before God as our Intercessor. The instrument of his priestly role is our human nature, united to his Godhead and loved by the Father. Out of that filial relationship comes our redemption. This preface is also found in the Roman Missal, where it is the 7th preface for the Sundays of Ordinary Time.

It is truly right and just, our duty and our salvation,
always, here and everywhere to give you thanks,
Lord, holy Father, almighty and eternal God.

In your mercy, you so loved the world
that you sent your Son as our Redeemer,
desiring that he should be like us in everything but sin,
so that you might love in us what you loved in your Son.
By our disobedience we lost your gifts of grace:
now through the obedience of Christ they are restored.

And so, Lord God, with angels and all saints
we exult and glorify your holy name:

Holy . . .

Sunday 13 and 28

'Hold in memory the wonderful works accomplished by your Son.' This is the rubric that governs every eucharist. What the works of Christ were, the eucharist is now for us: the gifts of liberation from death and an eternal inheritance.

It is truly right and just, our duty and our salvation,
always to give thanks to you, all-powerful and loving Father,
and hold in memory the wonderful work accomplished by
    your Son.

We celebrate the great mystery of our redemption
by which Christ has destroyed our slavery to death
and made us able to receive the gift of an eternal
    inheritance.

Through Christ the choirs of angels
worship forever with joy before your majesty;
with them, we pray you, join our voices
in this, their hymn of joyful supplication:

Holy . . .

Sunday 14 and 29

Redemption has the same origin as creation: it is found in the eternal wisdom of God.

It is truly right and just, our duty and our salvation,
to praise you, the all-powerful Father, in sincerity of heart;
because in wisdom you have found the means of our
   redemption
through the blood of Christ, your Son.

In boundless compassion you gave him to us
so that the human race created in your love,
yet fallen through its own pride,
might be restored to your glory
through his suffering and death upon the cross.

And so with joy we give you thanks
and acclaim your wonderful works
together with angels and saints
in this, their ageless hymn of praise:

Holy . . .

Sunday 15 and 30

*The eucharist is the sacrament of unity, enacting the 'gathering'
by Christ that forms the Church and makes it holy. While such
things are often said in the abstract, this preface is a reminder
that to speak of the eucharist is not to speak in a vacuum. It is
always 'this day's celebration' which is meant.*

It is truly right and just, our duty and our salvation,
always, here and everywhere to give you thanks,
Father all-powerful and merciful,
through Jesus Christ our Lord.

Christ your Son has called together
one holy people from every nation under heaven
and with love stronger than death
has embraced them as his own.
In the sacrament of Christ's body and blood
that work of salvation is made present
and accomplished for us in this celebration.

And so, Lord God, with angels and all saints
we exult and glorify your holy name:

Holy . . .

Sunday 16 and 31

With perhaps a recollection of Saint Luke's parable of the Good Samaritan (cf. Luke 10: 29–37), salvation is spoken of as healing from the wounds of sin and as life from death.

It is truly right and just, our duty and our salvation,
always, here and everywhere to give you thanks,
Lord, holy Father, almighty and eternal God.

Such is the abundance of your strong compassion
that you healed the wounds of our sins
and lifted us out of death into new and undying life.
You pour into our heart the Spirit of holiness,
to offer us the gift of a blessed resurrection
and an eternal destiny as your beloved sons and daughters.

And so, Lord God, with angels and all saints
we exult and glorify your holy name:

Holy . . .

Sunday 17 and the Weekdays of Week 32

Looking forward in Christian hope, this preface contrasts the present age with the age to come, earth with heaven. Sunday 32, the last Sunday of the year in the Ambrosian tradition, is the Solemnity of Christ the King.

It is truly right and just, our duty and our salvation,
always, here and everywhere to give you thanks,
Lord, holy Father, almighty and eternal God.

You have revealed to us our human destiny,
that we are born into this present world
to receive the gift of eternal life in your kingdom.
By the power of your word you fashioned us from earth
so that in tender love you might fill us
with the abundance of your heavenly gifts.

And so, with all the choirs of angels,
we praise your glory, now and for ever,
as with one voice we sing:

Holy . . .

Sunday 18

The preface for this Sunday returns to the theme of the restoration of humanity to its first dignity in the likeness of God.

It is truly right and just, our duty and our salvation,
always, here and everywhere to give you thanks,
Lord, holy Father, almighty and eternal God,
through Jesus Christ our Lord.

In Christ, eternal life is given to us
and our salvation is fully accomplished.
Christ has restored to its ancient beauty
your image and likeness in us,
that likeness created through him
yet marred by our sin;
and to complete his saving work
he has bestowed the promised gift of the Spirit.

Through Christ the choirs of angels
worship forever with joy before your majesty;
with them, we pray you, join our voices
in this, their hymn of joyful supplication:

Holy . . .

SAINTS' DAYS
THROUGHOUT THE YEAR

The Ambrosian Missal has a much larger number of proper prefaces for saints than does the Roman Sacramentary. The aim of these texts is both to celebrate and to teach.

In celebrating the saints, it is always the glory of the risen Christ that is the real object of celebration in the preface. The saints are Christ's followers and imitators; martyrs who share in his Passion or holy men and women who by their faith and mission make the love of God present in their own time.

As teaching documents, the prefaces draw on scripture or tradition to present a focussed portrait, something resembling an ikon in words. Inevitably, these portraits will be somewhat stylized and brief but their inclusion in the Eucharistic Prayer is itself a testimony to the way the Ambrosian tradition understands the Mystery of Salvation as an event constantly renewed in every age and culture through the life and example of these particular members of Christ's faithful people.

The Ambrosian Mass makes occasional provision also for reading from the Saint's life as part of the Liturgy of the Word, while in the Ambrosian Liturgy of the Hours there is always a brief biography of the saint recited at Vespers on the evening before the celebration of their feast.

Saint Antony the Abbot; 17 January

Antony was born around the middle of the third century and lived to nearly a hundred years of age, dying on 17 January 356. He is regarded as the founder of monasticism in the Church. His life, written by Saint Athanasius, tells how he heard the words of Jesus, 'Go, sell your possessions and give the money to the poor, then come and follow me'. He sought an increasing seclusion in the Egyptian desert, followed there by many disciples.

It is truly right and just, our duty and our salvation,
always, here and everywhere to give you thanks,
Lord, holy Father, almighty and eternal God,
and to offer you the sacrifice of praise
on this festival of the holy Abbot, Saint Antony.

You kindled in him the fire of your love,
so that with a singleminded joy
he heard and took to heart the precept of the Gospel.
Prompted by you, he gave up all he had,
and set his heart on following Christ alone.
Overcoming bodily weakness with vigour of spirit
this resolute seeker of solitude
chose the harshest wilderness to be his home.

And so, on his feast day
we join with him to adore you
and in the company of angels and saints
with whom he shares the vision of your glory
we proclaim your majesty in their joyful hymn of praise:

Holy . . .

Saint Sebastian, Martyr; 20 January

Saint Ambrose spoke of Sebastian as having been martyred under Diocletian's persecution. The famous images of young men being shot with arrows are absent from the preface for Saint Sebastian's feast. Absent also is most other information. Celebration, rather than teaching, is the focus here. This preface is also used, with the appropriate modifications, for the feast of Saint Lawrence.

It is truly right and just, our duty and our salvation,
always, here and everywhere to give you thanks,
Lord, holy Father, almighty and eternal God,
through Jesus Christ our Lord.

Christ revealed the depth of his love for us
by laying down his life for our redemption.
He taught that there is no greater love
than that which is poured out for you
and for our brothers and sisters.
Christ's martyr Sebastian
proved himself a true disciple of this teaching
and gave witness to that love even unto death.

Rejoicing in this gift of your loving kindness,
your Church rejoices with all the choirs of angels
in this, their glorious hymn of praise:

Holy . . .

Saint Agnes, Virgin and Martyr; 21 January

Agnes, a Roman martyr probably of the early fourth century, was praised by Saint Ambrose in a hymn celebrating virginity.

It is truly right and just, our duty and our salvation,
always, here and everywhere to give you thanks,
Lord, holy Father, almighty and eternal God,
as we celebrate the day you have made holy
through the martyrdom of Saint Agnes.

This is the day she entered
the company of Christ the eternal King.
She accepted death for professing his name,
and, just as she followed his footsteps in dying,
so now she is one with Christ in eternal glory.

Now, as we celebrate her memory
we join the host of angels and saints
in their exultant hymn of praise:

Holy . . .

Conversion of Saint Paul, Apostle; 25 January

This preface draws on the writings of Saint Paul to celebrate his feast.

It is truly right and just, our duty and our salvation,
always, here and everywhere to give you thanks,
Lord, holy Father, almighty and eternal God.

You displayed the wonders of your grace in your apostle
  Paul,
and chose him from his mother's womb
that in himself he should reveal your Son
and announce the good news to the gentiles.
He who had once been a blasphemer and persecutor
now showed himself so faithful in his ministry
that Christ Jesus himself made him
an example of patient service,
to instruct in the way of eternal life
all those who heard him and believed his word.

Now therefore, he who became your chosen instrument
for the salvation of the gentiles
has made us also eager to proclaim your mercy,
which we sing in union with all the powers of heaven
in this, their joyful hymn of praise:

Holy . . .

Saint Timothy and Saint Titus, Bishops;
26 January

*The Roman Rite also keeps this commemoration of Saint Paul's
two pupils and co-workers.*

It is truly right and just, our duty and our salvation,
always, here and everywhere to give you thanks,
Lord, holy Father, almighty and merciful God.

In your eternal and mysterious purpose of grace,
bestowed on us in Christ by your great mercy,
you have called us to holiness
and led us into lifegiving freedom.
In the Gospel of our Saviour you set before us
the depths of your wisdom and love.
You set apart Saint Timothy and Saint Titus
as preachers and apostles of that gospel
and as teachers of the gentiles.

Now, as we celebrate their memory
we join the host of angels and saints
in their exultant hymn of praise:

Holy . . .

Saint Thomas Aquinas, Priest and Doctor of the Church; 28 January

Born in about 1225, Thomas entered the new Order of Preachers (Dominicans) some time during his studies at Naples. He taught at the University of Paris and left behind him not just two massive theological systems, but the memory of himself as a faithful teacher, fed by an intense prayer life. He died in 1274.

It is truly right and just, our duty and our salvation,
always, here and everywhere to give you thanks,
Lord, holy Father, almighty and merciful God,
for you have given Saint Thomas to your Church
to teach the truth of the Catholic Faith.

He turned his back on wealth and honours
and opened his heart to the light of your word,
aspiring to teach with clarity and insight
what he had received in loving contemplation.
He yearned to study the wisdom of Christ,
and counted nothing more perfect or more pleasant.
He made it his life's great goal
that all his discourse should speak of you.
With ardent love he sought only Christ
by waiting on his Master by day and by night.
He found understanding of the mystery of Christ
which was his one desire, his one reward.

Now, as we celebrate his memory
we join the host of angels and saints
in their exultant hymn of praise:

Holy . . .

The Presentation of the Lord in the Temple; 2 February

The Preface for Candlemas in the Ambrosian Missal uses material from a Christmas preface which will be familiar. Together with the Christmas themes of some of the prefaces for the early Sundays of Ordinary Time, this allows the mystery of the Incarnation to colour the liturgy as far as Candlemas.

It is truly right and just, our duty and our salvation,
always, here and everywhere to give you thanks,
Lord, holy Father, almighty and eternal God.

Through the mystery of the Word made Flesh
you have shone with a new and radiant light
upon the eyes of mind and heart.
Christ your Son, who is one with you eternally,
was this day presented in the temple
and revealed by the Holy Spirit
as the glory of Israel and the Light of all peoples.

And so, with all the angels we give you glory
in this, their joyful hymn of praise:

Holy . . .

The Chair of Saint Peter, Apostle; 22 February

*On this celebration of the 'Chair' or teaching authority of Saint
Peter, this copious preface speaks of Peter's ministry in the light
of the whole history of salvation.*

It is truly right and just, our duty and our salvation,
always, here and everywhere to give you thanks,
Lord, holy Father, almighty and eternal God.

We praise you, the glory of your saints;
for by their holiness you establish and adorn
the Church, the body of Christ your Son.
In the old covenant, through patriarchs and prophets,
your wisdom prepared the way for your Church
which now, in these last times,
you have firmly founded on the apostles.
From their number you chose Saint Peter,
the first to profess faith in the divinity of Christ,
as that rock on which you would build your dwelling.
You made him guardian and leader of the flock,
to confirm his brothers and sisters in Christ.
Your Son entrusted to him the keys of the kingdom,
so that whatever he should bind on earth,
you, Father, would also bind in heaven.

And so, for the honour and glory you gave to Saint Peter
we celebrate this feast with all the choirs of angels
in this, their ageless hymn of praise:

Holy . . .

Saint Joseph, Husband of the Blessed Virgin Mary; 19 March

The Sacramentary provides two prefaces for this feast, the first of which resembles that found in the Roman Missal.

It is truly right and just, our duty and our salvation,
always, here and everywhere to give you thanks,
Lord, holy Father, almighty and eternal God,
as on this feast of Saint Joseph
we offer you our duty of praise and blessing.

He is that righteous man, given by you as husband
to Mary, the virgin Mother of God.
He is that wise and faithful servant
whom you placed over the household of Christ,
that with a father's love he might guard your Son
conceived by the overshadowing of the Holy Spirit.

As we celebrate the greatness of his calling
we glorify you with angels and saints
in this, their exultant hymn of praise:

Holy . . .

Saint Joseph, Husband of the Blessed Virgin Mary, 19 March

Second text

It is truly right and just, our duty and our salvation,
always, here and everywhere to give you thanks,
Lord, holy Father, almighty and eternal God.

We acknowledge your great and loving purpose
in committing the honour of Mary, virgin Mother of God,
into the care of Saint Joseph, righteous and faithful,
and placing under his watchful protection
your only Son our Saviour Jesus Christ.

Through Christ the whole creation rightly gives you praise
and the choirs of angels sing your glory.
With them we join our voices in this unceasing hymn:

Holy . . .

The Annunciation of the Lord; 25 March

This preface is the same as that found in the Roman Missal for this day.

It is truly right and just, our duty and our salvation,
always, here and everywhere to give you thanks,
Lord, holy Father, almighty and eternal God,
through Jesus Christ our Lord.

The Virgin Mary listened in faith
to the message of your angel
that the Holy Spirit would overshadow her
and that a son would be born for our salvation.
In her most pure womb she was to bear him,
so that your promise to the children of Israel
might in truth be fulfilled
and the hope of all the nations
be made real beyond all telling.

Through Christ the choirs of angels
worship forever with joy before your majesty;
with them, we pray you, join our voices
in this, their hymn of joyful supplication:

Holy . . .

Saint Peter of Verona, Presbyter, Martyr; 6 April

Peter of Verona belongs to one of the less salutary periods of the Church's activity. Born into a heterodox family at the beginning of the thirteenth century, Peter became a Catholic and entered the Dominican Order. The Milan region was the scene of intense activity in the combat against heretical groups, and Peter became a prominent advocate for the Church. On 6 April 1252 he was assassinated by heretics near Seveso. His death led to the conversion of his assassin and his body was buried where it is still venerated at the Milan Church of San Eustorgio.

It is truly right and just, our duty and our salvation,
always, here and everywhere to give you thanks,
Lord, holy Father, almighty and eternal God,
and to celebrate the birthday into eternal life
of your priest and martyr Saint Peter.

He stood forth as a faithful preacher of your name
and a steadfast opponent of those who taught error,
so that at the last he did not hesitate
to confirm his faith by the shedding of his blood.

Now, as we celebrate his memory
we join the host of angels and saints
in their exultant hymn of praise:

Holy . . .

Saint Mark, Evangelist; 25 April

The prefaces allotted to the four Evangelists celebrate aspects of their ministry. Here, Saint Mark's parable of the Sower is referred to as an image of the growth of the Gospel in the Church.

It is truly right and just, our duty and our salvation,
always, here and everywhere to give you thanks,
Lord, holy Father, almighty and eternal God,
through Jesus Christ our Lord.

You established that the mystery of our salvation
should be made known through holy scriptures,
the work of authors chosen and inspired
by the light of the Holy Spirit.
In this way, the words and deeds of the Saviour,
written in the pages of the eternal Gospel,
have been entrusted to the Church
to become a fertile seed
which bears the fruit of grace and glory for ever.

We who have received this Gospel with joy
unite with the choirs of angels and saints
to sing with one voice their joyful hymn of praise:

Holy . . .

Blessed Catherine and Juliana, Virgins; 27 April

Catherine was born near Milan at the beginning of the fifteenth century. After losing all her family to the plague, she joined a group of female hermits on the Sacro Monte at Varese. This became the nucleus of a hermit community recognized in 1474 by Pope Sixtus IV, whose Abbess she became two years later. As with many pious Catholics of the time, her spiritual life centred around the contemplation of Christ's passion. She died on 6 April 1478.

Juliana, a local woman who lived in the community as a lay sister, worked for the welfare of pilgrims and died in 1501.

It is truly right and just, our duty and our salvation,
always, here and everywhere to give you thanks,
Lord, holy Father, almighty and eternal God.

You gladden the heart of the poor and lowly
by this feast of blessed Catherine and Juliana,
whose lives you made radiant
with the light of innocence and the fire of love.
They vowed themselves to you
and consecrated themselves as virgins
in an unbreakable bond of love.
They sought from Christ his greatest gift,
to partake of the passion wherein he shed his blood.

And so with them and all the angels
we celebrate your glory
in this, their exultant hymn of praise:

Holy . . .

Saint Catherine of Siena, Virgin and Doctor of the Church; 29 April

Born in Siena in 1347, Catherine played a significant political and pastoral role in the Church of the late Middle Ages. Sent by the Republic of Florence as its ambassador to the Papal Court at Avignon, she persuaded Gregory XI to return to Rome. A great mystic, she died in Rome in 1380. She is the Patron Saint of Italy and was created Doctor of the Church by Paul VI in 1970.

It is truly right and just, our duty and our salvation,
always, here and everywhere to give you thanks,
Lord, holy Father, almighty and eternal God.

In this commemoration of Saint Catherine,
the holy virgin and doctor of your Church,
we praise you, Lord God, who drew her to yourself
and revealed to her the deepest mysteries of your life.
Through prayer and vigil she contemplated your beauty
and in the face of discord she called out for unity.
Obedient and lowly, she prayed for the Church of Christ,
that, mindful of his calling
the Church might show herself his faithful bride,
a spotless offering to you at the end of time.

And so, with her and all the angels and saints
we celebrate your glory
in this, their exultant hymn of praise:

Holy . . .

Saint Joseph, Worker; 1 May

The dignity of human labour is a frequent theme of recent Church teaching, and is the focus of this preface.

It is truly right and just, our duty and our salvation,
always, here and everywhere to give you thanks,
Lord, holy Father, almighty and eternal God.

In your providence you chose Saint Joseph
to be the guardian of your incarnate Son,
to bring him up with a father's love
and to be for your people a saving example,
a model and industrious craftsman.
Though born of David's royal line
he earned his bread in the sweat of his brow,
gracing his labours with holiness
in the company of Jesus and Mary.
To his trade he gave such nobility of spirit
that your only Son our Lord was not ashamed
to be called the Carpenter's son.

And so, with him and all the angels and saints
we celebrate your glory
in this, their exultant hymn of praise:

Holy . . .

Saint Philip and Saint James, Apostles; 3 May

Philip was one of the first to be called by Jesus. Ancient tradition records that he preached the Gospel in Phrygia, where at the age of 86 he was martyred.

James 'The Less' is venerated as the leader of the Jerusalem Church with the title 'Brother of the Lord' and is associated with the Letter bearing his name in the New Testament.

It is truly right and just, our duty and our salvation,
always, here and everywhere to give you thanks,
Lord, holy Father, almighty and eternal God,
as we celebrate the feast of your apostles Philip and James.

By your gracious call they became disciples of Christ
and followed his every deed and word,
desiring to know you, the Father, in fullness of truth.
Confirmed in faith by the resurrection of the Master,
they became steadfast and sure witnesses of salvation.
Now, in this assembly gathered for your glory,
we rejoice to share in that redemption
which you have given to the human race
and which their preaching has made known to us.

Now, as we celebrate their memory
we join the host of angels and saints
in their exultant hymn of praise:

Holy . . .

Saint Matthias, Apostle; 14 May

Matthias was elected by the apostles to take the place of Judas Iscariot. As one who had walked in their company with Christ, he was a fitting candidate for the apostolic office.

It is truly right and just, our duty and our salvation,
always, here and everywhere to give you thanks,
Lord, holy Father, almighty and eternal God.

With wisdom and love you looked on Saint Matthias
and chose him to complete the number of the apostles,
as one who had walked with your Son
and come to know the mystery of Christ.
You added his voice to the witness of the Twelve
to announce to the world that Christ was risen
and the heavenly kingdom prepared
for all men and women to enter.

Now, as we celebrate his memory
we join the host of angels and saints
in their exultant hymn of praise:

Holy . . .

Saint Dionysius, Bishop; 25 May

Dionysius was Ambrose's predecessor as Bishop of the Milanese Church. At a time when that Church was under pressure from the Arian heresy supported by the Emperor Constantius, Dionysius refused to sign an imperial decree condemning the Bishop of Alexandria, Athanasius. Sent into exile by the Emperor for his orthodox faith, he died far away in Armenia in 360 AD. Ambrose, having re-established Nicene orthodoxy in Milan, brought back the body of Dionysius to his own Church.

It is truly right and just, our duty and our salvation,
always, here and everywhere to give you thanks,
Lord, holy Father, almighty and eternal God,
and to honour the witness of Saint Dionysius your priest.

Unmoved by heresy or exile,
in the face of both he set forth your truth
and with steadfast heart kept faith with Christ your Son.
On this his feast day
we pay our homage of love and worship
and we acclaim your power, Lord God,
which gave him such strength and such resolve.

And so, with him and all your saints
we join to sing of your great glory
in this, their joyful hymn of praise:

Holy . . .

Saint Philip Neri, Presbyter; 26 May

*Born in Florence in 1515, as a young man he worked for the relief
of prisoners and the sick in Rome. Ordained presbyter at 36 years
of age, he founded the Oratory, at first a daily meeting to share
faith and participate in charitable work. He was remembered as
a particular friend of the young. He died on this day in 1595.*

It is truly right and just, our duty and our salvation,
always, here and everywhere to give you thanks,
Lord, holy Father, almighty and eternal God.

In Saint Philip you give us a bright example
and inspire us to be eager followers of Christ.
His witness gives a clear call to us
to love you always with cheerfulness
and serve you in our brothers and sisters
who are sick or in any kind of need.
His life has taught us
to cleave to you in simplicity of spirit
and come to know that such a lifelong sacrifice
is the offering that pleases you above all others.

Now, as we celebrate his memory
we join the host of angels and saints
in their exultant hymn of praise:

Holy . . .

Saint Vigilius, Bishop; Sisinius, Martyrius and Alexander, Martyrs; 29 May

This preface is also given for the feast of:

Saints Nabor and Felix (July 12)

and

Nazarius and Celsus (July 28)

A joint commemoration. Other prayers in the Ambrosian Missal and Liturgy of the Hours seem to be reluctant to treat Vigilius as a martyr, though sources elsewhere claim him as one. He is known as an early Bishop of Trent. Associated with him were Sisinius, Martyrius and Alexander, martyred in 397 AD in the Tyrol, where they had been sent to evangelize by Saint Ambrose.

It is truly right and just, our duty and our salvation,
always, here and everywhere to give you thanks,
Lord, holy Father, almighty and eternal God,
through Jesus Christ our Lord.

Glorified in heaven, Christ is the victorious Lamb
who calls martyrs to share in his triumph.
In the power of Christ's blood
Vigilius, Sisinius, Martyrius and Alexander
gave witness through many sufferings even unto death.
Now before your throne they stand,
their struggle accomplished,
their robes made white in the blood of the Lamb.
You, O God, will wipe away every tear from their eyes;
with living waters you will quench their thirst.
You grant them the glory of your name

and the name of Christ their Master
and a place among the citizens of the new Jerusalem.

Our voices join with theirs
and with all the powers of heaven
to glorify your holy name
in this, their ageless hymn of praise:

Holy . . .

The Visitation of the Blessed Virgin Mary; 31 May

The preface for this day celebrates two aspects of this feast: the gift of prophecy bestowed on Mary and on Elizabeth her kinswoman; together with Mary's act of love in visiting Elizabeth.

It is truly right and just, our duty and our salvation,
always, here and everywhere to give you thanks,
Lord, holy Father, almighty and eternal God,
through Jesus Christ our Lord.

Through the prophetic words of Elizabeth
inspired by the Holy Spirit,
you revealed to us the greatness
bestowed on the Virgin Mary.
Rightly is she greeted as the Blessed One
because she had believed the promise of salvation;
and, rightly welcomed for her kindly visit,
Mary is acclaimed as mother of the Lord
by her who is to be the mother of his herald.

And so, we join our voices
to the praises sung by the Mother of God
and in union with angels and saints
we glorify your holy name:

Holy . . .

Saint Justin, Martyr; 1 June

Born of a pagan family in Samaria at the beginning of the second century, Justin was a student of philosophy. At about thirty years of age he became a Christian and settled in Rome, where he taught. This preface takes lines from one of his two 'Apologiae' addressed to the Emperors Antoninus Pius and Marcus Aurelius, describing Christian faith and practice. Denounced by a rival philosopher as a Christian, he was martyred about the year 163 AD. An account of his martyrdom survives.

It is truly right and just, our duty and our salvation,
always, here and everywhere to give you thanks,
Lord, holy Father, almighty and eternal God.

In the beginnings of your Church
you chose Saint Justin as your witness,
to expound and defend in his writings
the mysteries of the prophets
and the teaching of the apostles
to Jew and gentile alike,
and to proclaim the Christian faith
before the mighty of this world.
For this devoted ministry you gave him the reward
of professing your faith in front of many witnesses,
even to the shedding of his blood.
You numbered him among the white-robed host of martyrs,
to receive the unfading crown of glory
at the hand of Christ the Lord.

And so, on his feast day
we join with him to adore you
and in the company of angels and saints
with whom he shares the vision of your glory
we proclaim your majesty in their joyful hymn of praise:

Holy . . .

Saint Barnabas, Apostle; 11 June

Barnabas, a levite of Cypriot origin 'full of the Holy Spirit and of faith' was the companion of Saint Paul, introducing him to the still distrustful Jerusalem community and accompanying him during his stay in Antioch and on his first missionary journey.

It is truly right and just, our duty and our salvation,
always, here and everywhere to give you thanks,
Lord, holy Father, almighty and eternal God.

By the voice of your Holy Spirit you chose Saint Barnabas
from the whole assembly of those who believed in Christ.
You numbered him among the apostles
as the companion of Saint Paul,
sending him to minister the truth of your Gospel
so that salvation and eternal life
might be announced to all the nations.

And so, on his feast day
we join with him to adore you
and in the company of angels and saints
with whom he shares the vision of your glory
we proclaim your majesty in their joyful hymn of praise:

Holy . . .

Saint Protase and Saint Gervase; 19 June

*These early martyrs of the Milanese Church were honoured by
Saint Ambrose, who translated their relics to the place he had
allotted for his own tomb in what is now the Basilica Di Sant'
Ambrogio.*

It is truly right and just, our duty and our salvation,
always, here and everywhere to give you thanks,
Lord, holy Father, almighty and eternal God,
through Jesus Christ our Lord.

You have given to all martyrs a strong and resolute faith
in the struggle they endured for love of your name.
Among them you have numbered the brothers
Saint Protase and Saint Gervase,
who, under the banner of the cross
took up the victorious armour
spoken of by your apostle,
and, freed from all earthly ties
were eager to follow Christ the Lord.
On this day the Church rejoices as a mother
because through Saint Ambrose she has recovered
the bodies of these her children,
strong witnesses to herself and pledges of your glory.

And so, on this their feast day
we join with them and all the powers of heaven
to glorify your holy name
in this, their joyful hymn of praise:

Holy . . .

Birth of Saint John the Baptist; 24 June: Vigil

The Ambrosian Missal provides two prefaces for this feast, one for the vigil and another for the day. In addition to these, the feast of the Passion of John the Baptist also has its own preface.

It is truly right and just, our duty and our salvation,
always, here and everywhere to give you thanks,
Lord, holy Father, almighty and eternal God,
and on this Birthday of Saint John the Baptist
to praise you for the wonders of your power.

His father Zechariah,
doubting the angel's promise of his birth,
lost the power of speech;
then, as John was born, his father's tongue was loosed
to sing and prophesy your praise and glory.
His mother Elizabeth, though old and childless,
you filled with the Holy Spirit,
so that in Mary her kinswoman
she recognized the mother of your only Son,
calling her blessed on account of her faith;
while in her own joyful womb
she felt the child leaping in exultation.

In that same joy with which you graced his birth
we now rejoice together with angels and saints
in this, their ageless hymn of praise:

Holy . . .

Birth of Saint John the Baptist; 24 June: Day

This preface takes as its theme the description of John by Jesus: John the last of the prophets, the greatest of all those born of women.

It is truly right and just, our duty and our salvation,
always, here and everywhere to give you thanks,
Lord, holy Father, almighty and eternal God,
especially on this day which you have made radiant
through the birth of Saint John the Baptist.

Before he was conceived you gave him his name;
before he was born you filled him with the Holy Spirit.
Though still in the womb,
he heard the voice of Christ's mother
and leapt with joy to acclaim the coming of the Saviour.
Christ the Lord knew him as the Forerunner
and among all those born of women
he counted him the greatest.

And so, for all the gifts
with which you endowed this great prophet,
we join with all the powers of heaven
in this, their joyful hymn of praise:

Holy . . .

Saint Arialdus, Deacon and Martyr; 27 June

Ordained deacon in his fiftieth year, Saint Arialdus was a vigorous reformer of his Church in an age of reform. Together with many others in the Church, he desired to promote celibacy for clergy and freedom from lay control for the Church. To express these ideas, Arialdus gathered around himself a community in order to live according to the Gospel. He was arrested and imprisoned by his enemies (not the least of whom was the Archbishop of Milan) and executed on this day in 1066.

It is truly right and just, our duty and our salvation,
always, here and everywhere to give you thanks,
Lord, holy Father, almighty and eternal God.

You call your people to celebrate
the memory of Saint Arialdus your deacon and martyr,
by whose example you give us the strength
to fight the good fight of faith.
Following the teaching of Saint Ambrose
and founded on the rock of the Apostle Peter,
this vigorous athlete of Christ
called back the ministers of your Son
to the dignity of a life lived in chastity.

Now, as we celebrate his memory
we join the host of angels and saints
in their exultant hymn of praise:

Holy . . .

Saint Peter and Saint Paul, Apostles;
29 June: Vigil

*Two prefaces are given for this feast, the first of which is also
found in the Roman Sacramentary as the preface for the day
itself.*

It is truly right and just, our duty and our salvation,
always, here and everywhere to give you thanks,
Lord, holy Father, almighty and eternal God.

Your holy Apostles, Saint Peter and Saint Paul,
fill us with praise for your plan of salvation.
Peter it was who first professed the faith
and Paul who unfolded it for our understanding.
Peter brought together the earliest Church
from the remnant of Israel's flock;
while Paul became your interpreter,
the teacher of gentiles whom you had called.
In differing ways they gathered one people for Christ;
one martyr's crown they shared
and are honoured as one throughout the world.

And so, Lord God, with angels and all saints
we exult and glorify your holy name:

Holy . . .

Saint Peter and Saint Paul, Apostles; 29 June: Day

The preface for the day speaks of God's grace as a turning point in the life of both Peter and Paul.

It is truly right and just, our duty and our salvation,
always, here and everywhere to give you thanks,
Lord, holy Father, almighty and eternal God,
and to praise you most of all on this day
when with joy we celebrate your apostles Peter and Paul.

You chose them both and set them apart:
you turned Saint Peter from his trade as a fisherman
to the preaching of your word;
and in Saint Paul your Church now rejoices
to have as her teacher of your commandments
the one who had been her fearsome persecutor.
To one you entrusted the keys of the kingdom of heaven;
the other you endowed with understanding of your Law
for the calling of gentiles into the Church.
You made them both bright lights in the apostles' fellowship
and as witnesses to the faith and love of Christ
you have crowned them for all eternity
with the radiance of your glory.

And so, in thanksgiving for their gifts
we praise you, the source of all good things,
as with angels and saints we adore you and say:

Holy . . .

The Immaculate Heart of the Blessed Virgin Mary; Saturday after the Second Sunday after Pentecost

The Feast of Christ's Sacred Heart is followed by that of his Mother. In becoming as it were the mother of the Beloved Disciple, she is also mother of all.

It is truly right and just, our duty and our salvation,
always, here and everywhere to give you thanks,
Lord, holy Father, almighty and eternal God,
through Jesus Christ our Lord.

As he hung upon the cross,
Christ entrusted his mother to John,
the beloved disciple,
to be a son to her in his place.
In this, the Lord revealed
not only love towards his mother
but a greater love, his purpose of salvation.
For John stands as a sign for all humankind
and as mother to John, Mary is mother of us all,
the bearer of Christ's love and grace in its fullness
to all who have known the rich treasures of her heart.

And so, with Mary and the whole assembly of saints
we add our voice to sing your glory
in this, their ceaseless hymn of praise:

Holy . . .

Saint Thomas, Apostle; 3 July

The Apostle who desired to touch in order to believe is here presented as an integral part of the divine plan. It was Christ's intention that he be absent, so as later to strengthen the faith of the remaining disciples in the resurrection.

It is truly right and just, our duty and our salvation,
always, here and everywhere to give you thanks,
Lord, holy Father, almighty and eternal God,
through Jesus Christ our Lord.

After his rising from the dead,
Christ appeared first to the disciples
in the absence of Thomas,
so that later, freed from the blindness of unbelief,
Thomas might touch the risen One
and so strengthen the faith of those who believe.
When this disciple acknowledged the true body of his
    Master,
he believed in him as his God and acclaimed him as his
    Lord,
becoming a faithful witness to the resurrection.

And so, with him and all the angels and saints
we celebrate your glory
in this, their exultant hymn of praise:

Holy . . .

Saint Benedict, Abbot; 11 July

Born about 480 AD, Benedict died on 21 March 547 AD. According to Gregory the Great, he became a hermit at Subiaco as a young man, disgusted with his contemporaries' lifestyle. Disciples gathered, however, and eventually Benedict settled at Monte Cassino, for which community he probably composed the 'Rule of Saint Benedict', with its emphasis on prayer, work and community life. Probably the most influential monastic figure after Saint Antony, Benedict was declared Patron of Europe in 1964 by Pope Paul VI.

It is truly right and just, our duty and our salvation,
always, here and everywhere to give you thanks,
Lord, holy Father, almighty and eternal God.

You bestowed on Saint Benedict
rich gifts of the Holy Spirit,
making him the father
of a great multitude of the just,
and an outstanding teacher
of love for you and for our neighbour.
In his holy Rule, with a clear and wise discretion,
he taught men and women to walk the path of salvation
under the guidance of Christ and the Gospel,
and now he is revered as the patron
of a multitude of nations.

And so, rejoicing in the glory you have given him,
we praise you with all the heavenly powers,
in this, their ageless hymn of praise:

Holy . . .

Saint Marcellina, Virgin; 17 July

Marcellina, sister of Saint Ambrose and Saint Satyrus his brother, was consecrated as a virgin by Pope Liberius, probably at Christmas of the year 353 AD. At her instigation, Ambrose wrote his celebrated work 'On Virginity'. Marcellina died about the year 400 AD.

It is truly right and just, our duty and our salvation,
always, here and everywhere to give you thanks,
Lord, holy Father, almighty and eternal God,
as today we celebrate with joy Saint Marcellina,
sister and consoler of Saint Ambrose and Saint Satyrus.

With the wisdom of an undivided heart
she chose the love of Christ your Son,
the giver of virginity,
and sinless child of a pure virgin.
She made herself his disciple and his bride,
and bound herself to celebrate his praises
in the midst of the Church.

Now, as we celebrate her memory
we join the host of angels and saints
in their exultant hymn of praise:

Holy . . .

Saint Mary Magdalen; 22 July

This preface honours Mary Magdalen as the first Evangelist and an inspiration for the eucharistic assembly celebrating her feast.

It is truly right and just, our duty and our salvation,
to praise you, the all-powerful Father, in every season,
and on this holy day to celebrate the glory
you gave to Saint Mary Magdalen.

You kindled in her heart a fire of love for Christ,
whose word had set her free
from the evil spirit that had oppressed her.
You gave her the courage of love,
to follow him even to the cross.
Seeking her Teacher after his death,
so great was her longing
that you made her the first
to behold him, risen from the dead,
and the first to announce to his apostles
that the Lord had risen to new and glorious life.
Her words still ring throughout the Church,
to strengthen the faith and encourage the hope
of those who gather faithfully for prayer.

And so with her, and all the citizens of heaven,
we join our voice to acclaim your glory
in this, their joyful hymn of praise:

Holy . . .

Saint James, Apostle; 25 July

James, son of Zebedee and brother of John, was a privileged witness to Christ. First to be called as a disciple, a witness both to the transfiguration and the agony in the garden, James was the first to suffer martyrdom.

It is truly right and just, our duty and our salvation,
always, here and everywhere to give you thanks,
Lord, holy Father, almighty and eternal God,
through Jesus Christ our Lord.

Christ called Saint James from mending fishing nets
to make him a fisherman of salvation
for men and women everywhere.
As James was ready and faithful in all things,
Christ made him the first among the apostles
to undergo the suffering
and receive the glory of a martyr's death.

And so, with him and all the angels and saints,
we celebrate your glory
in this, their exultant hymn of praise:

Holy . . .

Saint Joachim and Saint Anne, parents of the Blessed Virgin Mary; 26 July

The tradition that names Joachim and Anne as parents of Our Lady goes back to the second century A D. Legends of Mary's birth came to resemble those of Hannah in the Old Testament (a possible source for the name of Anne) and John the Baptist in the New.

It is truly right and just, our duty and our salvation,
always, here and everywhere to give you thanks,
Lord, holy Father, almighty and eternal God.

On this feast of Saint Joachim and Saint Anne
we glorify you, and in their memorial
we praise the loving purpose of your wisdom
which brought salvation to the human race.
You chose a people and called them to yourself
and made a covenant with them from of old.
By this you promised a new and fuller covenant,
to be made with all the peoples of the earth.
When the time came to fulfil that promise
you granted these parents a holy child, the Virgin Mary
through whom you gave us Christ to be our Saviour.

Now, as we celebrate their memory
we join the host of angels and saints
in their exultant hymn of praise:

Holy . . .

Saint Martha; 29 July

Mary and Martha of Bethany were the friends of Jesus and the
sisters of Lazarus whom he raised from the dead.

It is truly right and just, our duty and our salvation,
always, here and everywhere to give you thanks,
Lord, holy Father, almighty and eternal God.

On this feast of Saint Martha
we celebrate Christ the King of heaven,
whom she welcomed into her house
and served with great attentiveness.
For this generosity of heart
she obtained the resurrection of Lazarus her brother
from his four days' sojourn in death,
and now with Christ the Saviour, once her guest,
she is united for ever in the kingdom of heaven.

Now, as we celebrate her memory
we join the host of angels and saints
in their exultant hymn of praise:

Holy . . .

The Transfiguration of the Lord; 6 August

Before the eyes of Peter, James and John, Christ was transformed.
They saw his glory. This preface, found also in the Roman Missal,
is based on a sermon of Pope Leo the Great.

It is truly right and just, our duty and our salvation,
always, here and everywhere to give you thanks,
Lord, holy Father, almighty and eternal God,
through Jesus Christ our Lord.

Christ revealed his glory before chosen witnesses,
and filled with splendour
that human form in which he is one with us.
In this way he prepared the disciples
to bear the scandal of the cross
and showed that in the Church, his body,
that same glory would be fulfilled
that shone forth from him, its head.

And so, with all the choirs of angels,
we praise your glory, now and for ever,
as with one voice we sing:

Holy . . .

The Assumption of the Blessed Virgin Mary; 15 August

There are two masses for this feast; the first, a Vigil Mass for the evening of 14 August.

It is truly right and just, our duty and our salvation,
always, here and everywhere to give you thanks,
Lord, holy Father, almighty and eternal God.

We celebrate the day
when the holy Mother of God
underwent the death of the body
yet was not subject to the embrace of death;
for she had given birth in her own flesh
to your incarnate Son, our Lord.

United therefore with the choirs of angels,
we joyfully praise your glory and sing:

Holy . . .

The Assumption of the Blessed Virgin Mary;
15 August

*The second mass is for the day itself. This preface is the same as
the Roman Missal preface for the Assumption.*

It is truly right and just, our duty and our salvation,
always, here and everywhere to give you thanks,
Lord, holy Father, almighty and eternal God,
through Jesus Christ our Lord.

Today the virgin Mother of Christ
was taken up into the heavens,
to be the beginning and the likeness
of your Church in its fullness
and an assurance of hope and consolation
for your people on their pilgrim way.
You would not let her see corruption in the grave,
for she had given birth to your Son, the giver of life,
in the wonder of his incarnation.

United therefore with all the choirs of angels
we joyfully praise your glory and sing:

Holy . . .

The Blessed Virgin Mary, Queen; 22 August

22 August is the octave day of the Assumption of the Blessed Virgin Mary.

It is truly right and just, our duty and our salvation,
always, here and everywhere to give you thanks,
Lord, holy Father, almighty and eternal God,
through Jesus Christ our Lord.

You exalted the Mother of Christ
and crowned her in heaven with royal honours,
so that she might be a sign of your loving kindness
and a strong help for all your children.

For this privilege of the Mother of God
and for all the wonderful gifts of your love
we acclaim you in joy with the song of heaven's praise:

Holy . . .

Saint Bartholomew, Apostle; 24 August

It seems that we may identify the Nathanial of the Fourth Gospel with Saint Bartholomew. Saint John records his profession of faith (John 1:49). 'Rabbi, you are the Son of God. You are the King of Israel.' Tradition makes him the Apostle of India, and its first Christian martyr.

It is truly right and just, our duty and our salvation,
always, here and everywhere to give you thanks,
Lord, holy Father, almighty and eternal God.

We offer you this act of faith and worship
as we keep the festival of Saint Bartholomew the Apostle,
who followed the example of Christ his Master
and for his sake did not hesitate to shed his blood.
Doing battle in suffering, he gains the victor's palm
and to us he grants his own all-conquering faith.

And so, throughout the world
your people join to sing your glory
together with the powers of heaven
in this, their ageless hymn of praise:

Holy . . .

Saint Augustine, Bishop and Doctor of the Church; 28 August

One of the most memorable and accessible saints of the Catholic Church, Augustine was received into the Christian flock by Saint Ambrose, in Milan, at the Vigil of Easter 387 A D.

It is truly right and just, our duty and our salvation,
always, here and everywhere to give you thanks,
Lord, holy Father, almighty and eternal God.

In a wonderful way
you drew Saint Augustine to yourself,
and made him an outstanding witness
to glorify your grace,
and an inspiring teacher
to fill your Church with light.
You touched his heart with love for you
and filled him with zeal to proclaim your glory,
and so, by his faithful preaching of salvation
he gave nourishment to the flock committed to his care.

Now, as we celebrate his memory
we join the host of angels and saints
in their exultant hymn of praise:

Holy . . .

The Passion of Saint John the Baptist; 29 August

The forerunner of Christ both in life and in violent death is celebrated in this preface. In the Roman Missal it is the single preface for both feasts of Saint John the Baptist.

It is truly right and just, our duty and our salvation,
always, here and everywhere to give you thanks,
Lord, holy Father, almighty and eternal God,
through Jesus Christ our Lord.

In Christ's forerunner, Saint John the Baptist,
we praise your greatness which favoured him
with singular honour among those born of women.
Though his birth brought great rejoicing,
and while though yet unborn he leapt for joy
at the coming of our salvation,
it was John, alone among all the prophets
who revealed the Lamb, the world's Redeemer.
He baptized Christ, the giver of Baptism,
in waters which Christ had himself made holy;
then, at the last, he bore witness to Christ
by the shedding of his own blood.

Now, as we celebrate his memory
we join the host of angels and saints
in their exultant hymn of praise:

Holy . . .

The Birth of the Blessed Virgin Mary;
8 September

*The Church celebrates Mary's birth on this day, which was origin-
ally the dedication date of a church built in Jerusalem on the
reputed site of her birthplace. The Duomo of Milan is dedicated
to the Birthday of Our Lady.*

It is truly right and just, our duty and our salvation,
always, here and everywhere to give you thanks,
Lord, holy Father, almighty and eternal God.

We celebrate this radiant birthday,
when, like a wonderful bright star appearing,
the Mother of God, Mary pure and glorious,
was born into the world.
She has opened to us the gate of eternal life
which Eve in paradise had closed against us.
Through Christ her Son she leads us back
to the joyful light of our ancient home.

And so, with the Virgin Mary and all the saints
we join to sing the majesty of your glory
in this, their joyful hymn of praise:

Holy . . .

The Holy Name of Blessed Mary; 12 September

The ancient tradition of naming Mary as the 'Second Eve' is taken up in this preface.

It is truly right and just, our duty and our salvation,
always, here and everywhere to give you thanks,
Lord, holy Father, almighty and eternal God.

Rightly do we praise you
for your power shown forth in your saints,
and above all for the greatness
of blessed Mary the Virgin.
You bestowed on her the fullness of your grace,
that she might be for us the second Eve,
the Mother of your Son incarnate from heaven,
who came to destroy the powers of death
and restore to us eternal life.

And so, Lord God, with angels and all saints
we exult and glorify your holy name:

Holy . . .

The Exaltation of the Holy Cross; 14 September

The True Cross, by tradition discovered by Helena, mother of the Emperor Constantine, is celebrated today. The origin of this feast may be the dedication of Constantine's great Church of the Martyrium/Anastasis (now the Holy Sepulchre) in Jerusalem.

It is truly right and just, our duty and our salvation,
always, here and everywhere to give you thanks,
Lord, holy Father, almighty and eternal God,
through Jesus Christ our Lord.

We celebrate with songs of praise
the cross, the victory-sign of Christ.
Once through the fruit of the forbidden tree, we fell;
now through this tree Christ cancels all our guilt.
The power of this wood was once foretold
in the staff that Moses wonderfully uplifted
to open a saving passage through the waters
and drown the enemy beneath the waves.
On the tree of the cross our Redeemer hung,
becoming accursed for our sake,
to snatch us from our ancient foe
and lead us from death's dominion into eternal life.

And so with joy we give you thanks
and acclaim your wonderful works
together with angels and saints
in this, their ageless hymn of praise:

Holy . . .

The Blessed Virgin Mary of Sorrows; 15 September

The day after the Exaltation of the Cross comes the feast of the Mother of Sorrows. Medieval spirituality lost the sense of the cross as a triumph, and turned instead to its sorrowful aspect. The devotion to the Seven Sorrows of Our Lady became popular. This feast is a seventeenth-century creation, extended to the whole Church in 1814 during the Napoleonic Wars.

It is truly right and just, our duty and our salvation,
always, here and everywhere to give you thanks,
Lord, holy Father, almighty and eternal God,
through Jesus Christ our Lord.

As his holy body hung in torment on the cross
and a sharp sword pierced his virgin Mother's heart,
Christ freed the children of Adam
from subjection to the just sentence of death,
and with mercy led them back to eternal life.
In freely accepting death to take away our sins,
Christ willed that his holy Mother
should share in the sufferings of his passion,
so that through her intercession
his sacrifice might bear abundant fruit
among his faithful people.

And so, as we contemplate
the loving purpose of your wisdom,
we celebrate the help of our Mother's prayer
and glorify you with angels and saints:

Holy . . .

Saint Satyrus; 17 September

Uranius Satyrus was the brother of Saint Ambrose and Saint Marcellina. On his brother's election as Bishop of Milan, Satyrus joined him as the administrator of his household. After suffering shipwreck off Sardinia, he chose to be baptized. He died about the year 378 A D.

It is truly right and just, our duty and our salvation,
always, here and everywhere to give you thanks,
Lord, holy Father, almighty and eternal God.

In the wise purpose of your love
you gave Saint Satyrus, beloved brother of Saint Ambrose,
to be a companion to his brother
and a supporter of his ministry.
As a just and worthy steward of his household
he encouraged Ambrose in the priesthood
and by his chastity and poverty of spirit,
became a light to the growing Church of Milan.

And so, with him and all your saints
we join to sing of your great glory
in this, their joyful hymn of praise:

Holy . . .

Saint Matthew, Apostle and Evangelist; 21 September

Matthew, or Levi as he was known, was a tax collector called by Jesus to be his disciple. This preface remembers his conversion, as he welcomed Christ to eat at his table.

It is truly right and just, our duty and our salvation,
always, here and everywhere to give you thanks,
Lord, holy Father, almighty and eternal God.

In Christ your Son
you reveal your compassion for humankind
and in mercy you invite sinners
to sit at the banquet of your kingdom.
Saint Matthew responded to the call of Christ
and made him welcome in his house.
Changed and renewed by the coming of the Lord
he dedicated himself to proclaim
your wonderful works of salvation.

To his preaching of the Gospel
we respond with gladness,
joining all the powers of heaven
in this, their ceaseless hymn of praise:

Holy . . .

Saint Vincent De Paul, Presbyter; 27 September

Born in 1581 and ordained presbyter at the early age of 19, Vincent served the French Royal Family as Almoner to the Queen Mother, then abandoned court life and became a parish priest. In 1625 he founded the Congregation of the Mission, for evangelization, service of the poor and formation of priests. In 1633 together with Saint Louise De Marillac, he founded the Order of the Daughters of Charity. Vincent died in 1660.

It is truly right and just, our duty and our salvation,
always, here and everywhere to give you thanks,
Lord, holy Father, almighty and eternal God,
through Jesus Christ our Lord.

To the poor, Christ proclaimed mercy and salvation.
He desired to share completely in our human frailty,
humbling himself to be like us in all things.
Your servant Saint Vincent followed Christ
along this path of self-denial,
receiving the poor and afflicted
as his brothers and sisters
and giving witness before the world
to your boundless love for us.

Now, as we celebrate his memory
we join the host of angels and saints
in their exultant hymn of praise:

Holy . . .

Saint Michael, Gabriel and Raphael, Archangels; 29 September

Weaving together images from the Book of Daniel (7:10) and the Letter of Jude (verse 6) with Judaeo-Christian traditions, this preface celebrates the incorporeal angelic ministry towards God and towards humankind.

It is truly right and just, our duty and our salvation,
always, here and everywhere to give you thanks,
Lord, holy Father, almighty and eternal God.

As the glorious Lord of the universe,
you give life by your Word to bodiless creatures
to whom you allot the joyful ministry
of standing before your throne of glory.
When the rebellious spirits were cast into hell,
the host of angels and archangels
became your eternal crown of praise,
while carrying into your presence
our acts of worship, faith and prayer.

With them we hope to be fellow citizens of heaven,
but already on this earth we may bless you
in this, their ageless hymn of adoration:

Holy . . .

Saint Jerome, Presbyter and Doctor of the Church; 30 September

Born in Dalmatia in about 340 AD, Jerome received Baptism as a young man. Ordained and then made secretary to Pope Damasus, he later took up the life of a hermit in Bethlehem. His great work was the translation into Latin of the Bible, the so-called 'Vulgate', the standard western version of scripture for over a thousand years.

It is truly right and just, our duty and our salvation,
always, here and everywhere to give you thanks,
Lord, holy Father, almighty and eternal God,
and to praise the wonders of your wise counsel,
for by your word you have revealed to us
the mystery of our salvation.

You gave to Saint Jerome
gifts of insight into the scriptures,
from whose abundant riches
he drew things both new and old,
inspiring us by his example of devoted study
to seek in the words of scripture
the one true and living Word,
your Son, our Lord Jesus Christ.

And so with joy we acclaim your glory
and join the powers of heaven
in this, their exultant hymn of praise:

Holy . . .

Saint Thérèse of the Infant Jesus, Virgin;
1 October

Thérèse Martin was born at Alençon in 1873. At fifteen she entered the Carmelite Monastery in Lisieux, where she pursued a spirituality of what she called 'The Little Way' of childlikeness in heart. In 1895 she began to write her autobiography, which together with other notes and records leaves us a picture of a remarkable and strong young woman, who though dying of tuberculosis and sometimes afflicted with terrible depression, still clung to Christ as her example and her love.

It is truly right and just, our duty and our salvation,
always, here and everywhere to give you thanks,
Lord, holy Father, almighty and eternal God.

You reveal the secrets of your kingdom
to those who are counted as nothing by the world.
You called Saint Thérèse to follow you
in simplicity of life and devoted care for the Church.
In seeking complete faithfulness to you,
she has taught us to love you with all our strength
and daily to draw closer to you
by the practice of self-giving charity.

Now, as we celebrate her memory
we join the host of angels and saints
in their exultant hymn of praise:

Holy . . .

The Holy Guardian Angels; 2 October

Angels are messengers of God. God, however, is not just a message. God is the tender, all-encircling love that goes before us and follows us. The Guardian Angels' feast celebrates this truth about God.

It is truly right and just, our duty and our salvation,
always, here and everywhere to give you thanks,
Lord, holy Father, almighty and eternal God.

You reveal your wise purpose
for the salvation of the human race
by assigning to the angels
the ministry of your steadfast love.
While they contemplate your splendour and glory,
standing before you to sing your praise,
they also keep a faithful vigil for us
along the way that leads to life,
and guide us towards the kingdom of your light.

In joyful gladness we unite our voice with theirs
and sing the ageless hymn of your praise:

Holy . . .

Saint Francis of Assisi; 4 October

Francis was born in Assisi in 1132, the son of a wealthy merchant. As a young man he lived impetuously for riches and military honour, then, 'touched by grace', he changed and began to live a literal following of the Gospel in poverty. With twelve companions he began the Order of Friars Minor. After missionary work he spent the last years of his life in solitude, receiving the stigmata, the wounds of Christ, just before his death on 3 October 1226.

It is truly right and just, our duty and our salvation,
always, here and everywhere to give you thanks,
Lord, holy Father, almighty and eternal God,
through Jesus Christ our Lord.

From his fullness, Christ promised a hundredfold reward
for those who leave everything to be his disciples.
And so it was that in poverty
Saint Francis found the source of joy,
and strength in the simplicity
of loving you with all his heart.
He embraced the mystery of the cross
by freely accepting in his body
the wounds of his Master,
and gave new witness before the whole Church
to the abounding treasure of the Gospel.

And so, with all the angels and saints
we celebrate your glory
in this, their exultant hymn of praise:

Holy . . .

The Blessed Virgin Mary of the Rosary; 7 October

This feast originates as a thanksgiving for a naval victory over Turkish forces at Lepanto in 1571. That said, the military connection ends. This preface celebrates Mary as the Lord's Mother.

It is truly right and just, our duty and our salvation,
always, here and everywhere to give you thanks,
Lord, holy Father, almighty and eternal God,
and on this feast of blessed Mary, Ever-Virgin,
to praise and magnify your holy name.

In the saving work of Christ your Son
you gave her an honoured place
as the one who gave human birth to our Redeemer,
and to his people brings your strong help
on the way of salvation.

And so, with her and all the angels and saints
we celebrate the greatness of your glory
in this, their exultant hymn of praise:

Holy . . .

Saint Teresa of Avila, Virgin and Doctor of the Church; 15 October

With Saint John of the Cross, Teresa stands out as the great sixteenth-century reformer of her Carmelite religious community. Born in 1515, she founded thirty-two monasteries and left behind her a legacy of mystical spirituality. Teresa died on 4 October 1582. Paul VI named her a Doctor of the Church in 1970.

It is truly right and just, our duty and our salvation,
always, here and everywhere to give you thanks,
Lord, holy Father, almighty and eternal God.

You have revealed to us your kingdom
in the likeness of treasure lying buried in a field.
You gave to Saint Teresa the blessing of finding it
and selling all to purchase this greatest of delights.
As a wise teacher of your word,
she brought forth from its riches
things both new and old,
and as a provident and faithful servant
she fed your Church with the nourishment of truth.

Now, as we celebrate her memory
we join the host of angels and saints
in their exultant hymn of praise:

Holy . . .

Blessed Contardo Ferrini; 16 October

Contardo Ferrini was a Milanese born in 1859. After studying Law in Pavia and Berlin, he taught in the universities of Messina, Modena and Pavia. As well as teaching, he was active in promoting the cause of the poor in his native city. He adopted the celibate life, in which he practised daily meditation, prayer and reception of the sacrament. He died in 1902.

It is truly right and just, our duty and our salvation,
always, here and everywhere to give you thanks,
Lord, holy Father, almighty and eternal God.

We praise you for your servant blessed Contardo Ferrini,
an example of that Christian faith and wisdom
which leads to Christ, the radiance of your glory
and sole fountain of life.
You opened to this man your inner life
which he followed each day
with the longing of earnest prayer.
Strong in faith, a servant of your truth;
before the world he taught the Christian life,
worked for justice and sought your glory above all else.

And so, with angels and all the powers of heaven
we bless your steadfast love
in their unceasing hymn of praise:

Holy . . .

Saint Luke, Evangelist; 18 October

Luke, a Greek convert, was the companion of Saint Paul on his second and third missionary journeys. The tradition of the Church ascribes to him both the Gospel that bears his name and the Acts of the Apostles.

It is truly right and just, our duty and our salvation,
always, here and everywhere to give you thanks,
Lord, holy Father, almighty and eternal God,
through Jesus Christ our Lord.

You willed that the mystery of Christ your Son
should be made known to us through scriptures,
the work of those you enlightened by the Holy Spirit.
These have entrusted to your Church
the words and acts of the Saviour
in writings that will endure
to be a fertile seed for all generations
bearing rich fruit to your praise and glory.

With these holy Gospels to inspire us
we join the choirs of angels and saints
in this, their joyful hymn of praise:

Holy . . .

Saint Simon and Saint Jude, Apostles; 28 October

*Simon the Zealot and Jude also known as Thaddeus are com-
memorated together in the Latin rites. This preface is found in
the Roman Sacramentary as the preface for all apostles' feasts.*

It is truly right and just, our duty and our salvation,
always, here and everywhere to give you thanks,
Lord, holy Father, almighty and eternal God.

You, the eternal Shepherd,
will never forsake your flock;
but through the holy apostles
you keep it under your continual protection;
so that your people may always be led by those
whom you have called to stand in the place of your Son
as shepherds at your Church's head.

Therefore with angels and saints
we sing the unceasing hymn of your glory:

Holy . . .

All Saints; 1 November

This feast was originally the dedication of the Roman Church of Saint Mary of the Martyrs, formerly the Pantheon, a pagan temple dedicated to all the gods. This preface, found also in the Roman Sacramentary, celebrates the glory of the heavenly Jerusalem.

It is truly right and just, our duty and our salvation,
always, here and everywhere to give you thanks,
Lord, holy Father, almighty and eternal God.

Today you gather your Church
to keep the festival of your holy city,
that heavenly Jerusalem which is our mother.
Within her walls the saints, our brothers and sisters,
crown you with praise for all eternity.
Towards them we hasten with eager steps
as pilgrims who walk by faith,
rejoicing in the glory you have given
to these members of your Church,
whose radiance also you display before us
to strengthen and inspire our weakness here on earth.

And so, with all the company of saints and angels
we glorify you in their hymn of praise:

Holy . . .

Saint Charles Borromeo, Bishop; 4 November

Saint Charles, Archbishop of Milan from 1565, was an outstanding figure in the reform of the Catholic Church at the time of the Council of Trent. He encouraged both diocesan clergy and religious houses in reform and renewal of discipline. His work during outbreaks of plague in Milan was noteworthy, as he set an example to his priests by administering the last sacraments with his own hands. He died on pilgrimage to the Sacro Monte Di Varallo on 3 November 1584.

It is truly right and just, our duty and our salvation,
always, here and everywhere to give you thanks,
Lord, holy Father, almighty and eternal God,
in this commemoration of your bishop Saint Charles
whose ministry you have so gloriously rewarded.

You gave him to the Church as a vigilant pastor,
a lamp shining your light in the darkness of this world,
a priest fired by the immensity of Christ's love;
a mirror of strength, a pattern of justice for the flock.
By your generous gift he led your sheep
with diligent care safely to the sheepfold,
and in days of trial and danger
sustained them with zeal and love.

As we recall the memory of this great bishop,
we stand before you, together with the angels,
to join in their unending hymn of praise:

Holy . . .

Saint Martin of Tours, Bishop; 11 November

Saint Martin is one of the first great missionary bishops of the western Church. Born about 316 AD and destined for a military career, he rejected this and instead became a monk first in Gaul and later in Milan, whence he was expelled by the Arian bishop Auxentius. In 371 he was elected as Bishop of Tours, where he remained for twenty-six years, as the Ambrosian Liturgy of the Hours describes him: 'Soldier, monk, bishop, evangelizer and friend of the poor.'

It is truly right and just, our duty and our salvation,
always, here and everywhere to give you thanks,
Lord, holy Father, almighty and eternal God,
as we praise you for the example of Saint Martin,
a glorious servant of Christ your Son.

He prepared eagerly to receive the grace of baptism
by showing an exemplary love for the poor.
He rejected the rewards of military service
in order to serve Christ, the only true Lord,
in the humble pursuit of monastic life.
Chosen by you as bishop of your flock,
zealous for the true faith and love of the Church,
Martin became a model of spiritual strength for all.

And so, with all the citizens of heaven
we join with him to acclaim your glory
in this, their ageless hymn of praise:

Holy . . .

Saint Andrew, Apostle; 30 November

According to Saint John's Gospel, Andrew was a disciple of John
the Baptist. After John's witness to Jesus as the Lamb of God,
Andrew followed Jesus and brought his own brother, Simon Peter,
into the company of the Lord. Ancient tradition records that
Saint Andrew preached the Gospel and suffered martyrdom by
crucifixion in Achaia.

It is truly right and just, our duty and our salvation,
always, here and everywhere to give you thanks,
Lord, holy Father, almighty and eternal God.

In this great mystery of our salvation
we celebrate today Saint Andrew,
who by his preaching of Christ, your Son,
and by the witness of his martyrdom,
showed himself a true brother
to your apostle Saint Peter
and shared in the suffering and the glory
of all those called by Christ as his apostles.

And so, on his feast day
we join with him to adore you
and in the company of angels and saints
with whom he shares the vision of your glory
we proclaim your majesty in their joyful hymn of praise:

Holy . . .

The Ordination of Saint Ambrose, Bishop and Doctor of the Church; 7 December: Vigil Mass

Ambrose was born at Trier in about 340 AD and distinguished himself in the imperial service as Governor in Milan. Still a catechumen, he was elected Bishop of Milan by popular acclamation in 374 and ordained on this day. One of the greatest bishops of the Latin Church, he gives his name to the whole Milanese liturgical tradition.

The Ambrosian Rite celebrates its great bishop with two masses, a vigil and a day mass. The vigil mass preface is almost identical to that found in the Roman Missal as the Preface of Pastors.

It is truly right and just, our duty and our salvation,
always, here and everywhere to give you thanks,
Lord, holy Father, almighty and eternal God,
through Jesus Christ our Lord.

You gather your Church
to celebrate this feast of Saint Ambrose,
so that you may bless your people
with strength from his example of service,
wisdom from his preaching
and protection through his constant prayer.

And so, with all the angels we give you glory
in this, their joyful hymn of praise:

Holy . . .

The Ordination of Saint Ambrose, Bishop and Doctor of the Church; 7 December. Day Mass.

It is truly right and just, our duty and our salvation,
always, here and everywhere to give you thanks,
Lord, holy Father, almighty and eternal God.

In your holy Catholic Church
you ordain your priests and order their ministry
to make your Church a flawless bride for Christ your Son.
This is the day of our solemn festival,
when you raised your disciple Saint Ambrose
to the dignity and seat of a Bishop.
You set aside the symbols of his public office
and made him the teacher and the judge of your flock,
confirming his ministry as the pastor of your Church.

And so, on his feast day
we join with him to adore you
and in the company of angels and saints
with whom he shares the vision of your glory
we proclaim your majesty in their joyful hymn of praise:

Holy . . .

The Immaculate Conception of the Blessed Virgin Mary; 8 December

This preface in praise of Mary sees her as the archetype of the Church, as the testimony to the unique intervention of God for salvation and as our pattern of holiness.

It is truly right and just, our duty and our salvation,
always, here and everywhere to give you thanks,
Lord, holy Father, almighty and eternal God.

You kept the Blessed Virgin Mary
free from the mark of original sin;
you endowed her with the fullness of your grace
so as to make her a worthy mother of your Son.
In Mary, you mark the beginning of your Church,
which is to be presented to Christ
as his fair and spotless bride.
Purest of virgins, she was to bear your Son,
the innocent Lamb who takes away our sins.
You chose her before all other women
to be for your people an advocate of grace
and a pattern of holiness.

We therefore, your people bound to her in love,
give thanks for the glory of our blessed Mother
and together with the powers of heaven we praise you
in their unceasing hymn of adoration:

Holy . . .

VARIOUS OCCASIONS

Five collections of mass texts conclude the Ambrosian Missal:

1. *'Commons', i.e., mass texts common and applicable to different kinds of saint's day or other celebration.*
2. *'Ritual Masses' – those masses that accompany other celebrations such as Baptism or Confirmation.*
3. *Masses for various needs and occasions in the life of the Church or civil society.*
4. *'Votive Masses', i.e., masses celebrated in honour of the mystery of salvation or a saint, but not linked to the course of the Church's annual cycle.*
5. *Masses for the Dead: funerals and commemorations.*

Many of these masses have their own preface. Some use prefaces found elsewhere in the Missal.

COMMONS

Common of the Dedication of a Church:
Anniversary of Dedication 1: in the Church itself

*This preface celebrates the Church as a visible place signifying
the unseen communion of God with his people.*

It is truly right and just, our duty and our salvation,
always, here and everywhere to give you thanks,
Lord, holy Father, almighty and eternal God,
through Jesus Christ our Lord.

You allow us to build this visible dwelling
where you never cease to encourage your people
on their pilgrimage towards you.
Here in sacramental signs
you manifest and accomplish
the mystery of your communion with us.
Here also you build up that temple which is ourselves;
until your Church throughout the world
grows into the one body of Christ our Lord,
reaching its fullness in the vision of peace
that is your heavenly city, the new Jerusalem.

And so, with all who dwell in that same city,
we glorify your holy name
in this, their ageless hymn of praise:

Holy . . .

Common of the Dedication of a Church: Anniversary of Dedication 2: outside the Church itself

Seen and unseen, of this age and of the age to come; such is the mystery of Christ's Church.

It is truly right and just for us to give you thanks,
to bless and praise you, here and everywhere,
almighty and eternal God.

You are pleased to make your home
in every house of prayer,
and by the ceaseless action of your grace
you make us the temple of your Spirit,
whose beauty is the splendour
of lives wholly dedicated to you.
In houses of prayer
you give a sign of the Church on earth
and by the working of that same Spirit
you hallow your Church as the bride of Christ,
so that as the joyful mother of countless children
she may be given a place amid your glory
in the kingdom of heaven.

Therefore with angels and saints
we sing the unceasing hymn of your glory:

Holy . . .

Common of the Blessed Virgin Mary 1

This preface is also that of the First Sunday of Ordinary Time.

Common of the Blessed Virgin Mary 2

'By the grace of Christ her Son' Mary's glory is to be the Mother of Christ.

It is truly right and just, our duty and our salvation,
always, here and everywhere to give you thanks,
Lord, holy Father, almighty and eternal God.

As we commemorate the Blessed Virgin Mary
we honour you with fitting praise,
since in your eternal plan of salvation
you exalted her above all you have created.
By the grace of her Son
she was most wonderfully redeemed,
her whole destiny united to him
in a unique and unbreakable bond.
You gave her the highest honour,
choosing her as the Ever-Virgin Mother of your only Son,
as your daughter most beloved
and the temple of the Holy Spirit.

And so, Lord God, with angels and all saints
we exult and glorify your holy name:

Holy . . .

Common of the Blessed Virgin Mary 3

An ancient Christian tradition names Mary as the Second Eve,
mother of believers, through a new and heavenly birth.

It is truly right and just, our duty and our salvation,
always, here and everywhere to give you thanks,
Lord, holy Father, almighty and eternal God.

Rightly do we desire to praise you
for the glory of all your saints,
but most especially for the greatness
of the Blessed Virgin Mary.
With grace in its fullness you honoured her,
that she should be for us the Second Eve,
and that through her Son
a new and heavenly birth might be ours,
in which death itself should die
and eternal life be restored to us.

And so, Lord God, with angels and all saints
we exult and glorify your holy name:

Holy . . .

Common of the Blessed Virgin Mary 4: Advent Season

This preface is the same as that given for the Sixth Sunday of Advent (first text).

Common of the Blessed Virgin Mary 5: Christmas Season

Mary, Virgin and Mother: 'A marvel surpassing all our power to tell.'

It is truly right and just, our duty and our salvation,
always, here and everywhere to give you thanks,
Lord, holy Father, almighty and eternal God.

In the holiness of blessed Mary
you have taught us to cherish a wonderful mystery,
a marvel surpassing all our power to tell.
For she, though Mother, yet remained a virgin,
chaste and faithful in body and heart.
In this did she know herself as Mother of the Lord:
that the angel's word brought her joy, not shame;
and while she marvelled at her childbearing,
she rejoiced that she had borne our Redeemer.

Through Christ the choirs of angels
worship forever with joy before your majesty;
with them, we pray you, join our voices
in this, their hymn of joyful supplication:

Holy . . .

Common of the Blessed Virgin Mary 6:
Easter Season

A preface echoing the Magnificat, praising the steadfast love of God. In the Roman Missal this preface is the second common preface of the Virgin Mary.

It is truly right and just, our duty and our salvation,
to proclaim the wonders which you, our Father,
have worked in all your saints;
and in commemorating the Blessed Virgin Mary
to sing with her in praise of your holy name,
glorifying your power and steadfast love.

Truly, you work wonders over all the earth;
and from age to age you extend your gracious mercy.
You looked with favour on your lowly servant
and through her you gave to the world
Jesus Christ your Son our Lord,
the author of salvation for humankind.

And so, Lord God, with angels and all saints
we exult and glorify your holy name:

Holy . . .

Common of the Blessed Virgin Mary 7:
Saint Mary Mother of the Church

Mother of Christians, exemplar of prayer, Mary awaits the pilgrim Church in heaven.

It is truly right and just, our duty and our salvation,
always, here and everywhere to give you thanks,
Lord, holy Father, almighty and eternal God,
and in celebration of the Blessed Virgin Mary
to give you glory and fitting praise.

As she stood by the cross of Jesus
she accepted her Son's last gift of love
and took to herself, as her own children,
all those who by the death of Christ
are born again to eternal life.
She joined in prayer with the apostles
to await the coming of your Promised Spirit
and so she becomes for us
the perfect model of the Church at prayer.
Raised to the eternal glory of heaven,
she watches over your pilgrim people
with a mother's affection,
and follows their journey homeward,
until the day of the Lord dawns in splendour.

And so, with saints and angels we glorify you
in this, their ageless hymn of praise:

Holy . . .

Common of Martyrs 1: One Martyr

The martyr shares in the Passion of Christ.
Masculine pronouns, which the Latin uses exclusively, are
rendered throughout this section as such, but in italics.

It is truly right and just, our duty and our salvation,
always, here and everywhere to give you thanks,
Lord, holy Father, almighty and eternal God.

Your holy martyr N. took strength from you
to undergo *his* torment with courage
and shrank not from the struggle
of suffering death for the sake of your name.
And so, through shedding *his* blood
he became a true follower
of the passion of Christ your Son.
He left this world of transient light
for a blessed and eternal home,
and there *he* has received an unfading crown
of light that shines for all eternity.

Now, as we celebrate *his* memory
we join the host of angels and saints
in their exultant hymn of praise:

Holy . . .

Common of Martyrs 2: One Martyr

The martyr as a witness to Christ's resurrection.

It is truly right and just, our duty and our salvation,
always, here and everywhere to give you thanks,
Lord, holy Father, almighty and eternal God,
through Jesus Christ our Lord.

Christ called his martyr N. into glory
and through the wounds of *his* martyrdom
led *him* to the palm of a heavenly reward.
As Christ's true witness in holiness
he freely laid down *his* life to die for Christ,
knowing that in glory *his* body would arise.
He chose to die to this world
rather than to be separated from Christ,
perceiving that here *he* had no abiding city
but looked for an unfading inheritance in heaven.

And so, on *his* feast day
we join with *him* to adore you
and in the company of angels and saints
with whom he shares the vision of your glory
we proclaim your majesty in their joyful hymn of praise:

Holy . . .

Common of Martyrs 3: One Martyr

The martyr as example of Christian witness.

It is truly right and just, our duty and our salvation,
always, here and everywhere to give you thanks,
Lord, holy Father, almighty and eternal God.
We praise your power, revealed in 'N. your martyr,
whose prayer you granted,
that *he* might find eternal happiness with you.

Joyfully *he* accomplished the close of *his* earthly life
as a Christian both in name and in deed.
And so, after suffering death *he* rises to freedom in you,
in you *he* is reborn to new and heavenly life.
The love of Christ drew *him* with such power,
that as a faithful disciple *he* let no-one hinder *him*
from following the way of Christ *his* Master,
as the pattern and reward for *his* sacrifice.

Now, as we celebrate *his* memory
we join the host of angels and saints
in their exultant hymn of praise:

Holy . . .

Common of Martyrs 4: Missionary Martyr

The martyr's example is Christ, who died to gather the scattered children of God.

It is truly right and just, our duty and our salvation,
always, here and everywhere to give you thanks,
Lord, holy Father, almighty and eternal God,
through Jesus Christ our Lord.

Christ laid down his life in perfect love,
dying not only for his own nation
but to gather all your scattered children into one.
Christ's faithful servant and disciple Saint N.
shared *his* Master's destiny with joy,
and for the sake of Christ's name
bore hatred and persecution without fear.
Strengthened by the Holy Spirit
who gave witness to Christ within *his* heart,
he also was established as a witness to the Master.

Now, as we celebrate *his* memory
we join the host of angels and saints
in their exultant hymn of praise:

Holy . . .

Common of Martyrs 5: a Virgin Martyr

The martyr, a bride of Christ.

It is truly right and just, our duty and our salvation,
always, here and everywhere to give you thanks,
Lord, holy Father, almighty and eternal God,
as we celebrate the day
when Saint N. received the martyr's blessed crown.

She consecrated herself as a bride to Christ
in fidelity of heart and the shedding of her blood
and as a virgin achieved the martyr's death.
Christ, the pure offspring of a holy Virgin,
drew her with such a surpassing love
that, remaining chaste in body and spirit,
she bore without fear both torment and death
for the sake of his name.

Rejoicing for her, now glorified in heaven,
with angels and saints we acknowledge you as Lord
and sing the ageless hymn of your praise:

Holy . . .

Common of Martyrs 6: Several Martyrs

'Chosen from the beginning' (cf. Ephesians 1:4) to bring glory to God.

It is truly right and just, our duty and our salvation,
always, here and everywhere to give you thanks,
Lord, holy Father, almighty and eternal God;
and to praise the wonder of your work
revealed in N. and N. your martyrs.

Before the foundation of the universe
you chose them in Christ as your witnesses,
to glorify your name
and reveal before the world your light of truth.
By the Holy Spirit you gave them great courage
so that in the very weakness of this mortal body
they might conquer death and overcome its power.

And so, on this their feast day
we join with them and all the powers of heaven
to glorify your holy name
in this, their joyful hymn of praise:

Holy . . .

Common of Martyrs 7: Several Martyrs

The Church is glorified through her martyrs.

It is truly right and just, our duty and our salvation,
always, here and everywhere to give you thanks,
Lord, holy Father, almighty and eternal God,
through Jesus Christ our Lord.

As we celebrate the feast of your martyrs N. and N.,
we praise Christ, who kindles the fire of love
in the heart of his faithful servants,
so that they renounce the honours of this world
and by martyrdom take their place
amid the citizens of heaven.
By their sufferings your Church is made holy and glorious
and placed with Christ at your right hand.
Her joy and radiance is the prayer of her martyrs,
persecuted in this world,
whom she presents to you
as the firstfruits of the world to come.

And so, throughout the heavens and the earth
all things adore you and sing a new song;
and we with all the angels give you glory
in this, their ever-joyful hymn of praise:

Holy . . .

Common of Pastors 1: for a Pope

The example of Saint Peter's faith.

It is truly right and just, our duty and our salvation,
always, here and everywhere to give you thanks,
Lord, holy Father, almighty and eternal God,
through Jesus Christ our Lord.

Three times the Lord asked Peter if he loved him,
before finding him worthy to be the Shepherd of his sheep.
In succession to Peter, Christ chose Saint N.,
to be Bishop of the Roman Church,
to preside in love over the whole assembly of believers
and, made strong in faith himself,
to strengthen the faith of his brothers and sisters.

And so, with all the angels we give you glory
in this, their joyful hymn of praise:

Holy . . .

Common of Pastors 2: for a Bishop of the Milanese Church

A celebration of the local Church, gathered for the eucharist around its Bishop.

It is truly right and just, our duty and our salvation,
always, here and everywhere to give you thanks,
Lord, holy Father, almighty and eternal God.

This joyful community of faith,
your new people, filled with the gifts of the Spirit,
assembles together in union with our Bishop
to celebrate the memory of Saint N., Bishop of Milan.
Here by your mercy we gather,
all those you have chosen and called to be your children.
Here before us the Gospel is preached
and the one fellowship of charity
fulfilled in the Supper of the Lord,
to make your Church a sign of love and unity for all.

And so with heartfelt joy and gladness,
we join the powers of heaven
in their exultant hymn of praise:

Holy . . .

Common of Pastors 3: for a Bishop

Christ, the chief Shepherd, chooses the shepherds of the flock.

It is truly right and just, our duty and our salvation,
always, here and everywhere to give you thanks,
Lord, holy Father, almighty and eternal God,
through Jesus Christ our Lord.

Christ is the Good Shepherd of the whole flock,
in which the Holy Spirit has ordained bishops
to govern the Church bought by the blood of Christ.
In Saint N., your servant and Bishop,
Christ the Shepherd found a faithful disciple,
chosen after your own heart's desire
to be an example for the flock;
a minister, not for his own profit
but for the wellbeing of your inheritance.

Now, crowned with glory unfading,
he gives praise to you in company with the angels,
who sing with us this joyful hymn of your glory:

Holy . . .

Common of Pastors 4: for a Bishop or Presbyter

A good steward, commended by his master.

It is truly right and just, our duty and our salvation,
always, here and everywhere to give you thanks,
Lord, holy Father, almighty and eternal God,
worthy indeed of the highest glory
for the witness of your Bishop/Priest Saint N.

For praiseworthy lives you give a great reward;
you call those who have served you in holiness
as ministers of your Church
to enter into the joy of their Master.
And so, as Saint N. was found faithful in small things
during the course of this earthly life,
you have given into his keeping
those great and eternal good things
prepared for those who love you.

Now, as we celebrate his memory
we join the host of angels and saints
in their exultant hymn of praise:

Holy . . .

Common of Pastors 5: for a Presbyter

The ministry of priests is to gather and sanctify the Church,
revealing it to the world as the sacrament of salvation.

It is truly right and just, our duty and our salvation,
always, here and everywhere to give you thanks,
Lord, holy Father, almighty and eternal God,
as we honour the memory of your priest, Saint N.

Your wise purpose set him apart in your Church
that by his daily service
it might grow in spirit as the body of Christ.
To your children he faithfully proclaimed
the good news of salvation
and gave them nourishment
by celebrating the sacred mysteries,
so that he might reveal them to the world
as a people called to share your grace
through communion in the one true faith
and in the work of sincere charity.

And so, on his feast day
we join with him to adore you
and in the company of angels and saints
with whom he shares the vision of your glory
we proclaim your majesty in their joyful hymn of praise:

Holy . . .

Common of Pastors 6: for a Missionary

The Missionary Church: 'Sacrament of Salvation' for all peoples of the earth.

It is truly right and just, our duty and our salvation,
always, here and everywhere to give you thanks,
Lord, holy Father, almighty and eternal God,
through Jesus Christ our Lord.

Christ founded the Church as the sacrament of salvation,
and sent forth apostles to announce the good news
and make all nations disciples of his teaching.
With eager heart, Saint N. followed their example;
and through *his* ministry
your Church has been made known
to peoples and nations,
opening the way in surety and freedom
towards a sharing in the lifegiving mystery of Christ.

And so, on *his* feast day
we join with *him* to adore you
and in the company of angels and saints
with whom *he* shares the vision of your glory
we proclaim your majesty in their joyful hymn of praise:

Holy . . .

Common of Pastors 7: for a Missionary

The Missionary Church: a minister to make the nations an acceptable sacrifice to God.

It is truly right and just, our duty and our salvation,
always, here and everywhere to give you thanks,
Lord, holy Father, almighty and eternal God,
through Jesus Christ our Lord.

Christ has never ceased to call his disciples;
he sends them out to bring salvation to the nations
by the light of the Gospel.
For this work, Saint N. was set apart by the Spirit;
in faith and obedience *he* went to peoples far away.
You called *him* to be all things to everyone
as a minister of your word, O most High,
so that in your sight the nations might become
a holy sacrifice, acceptable to you.

And so, with *him* and all your saints
we join to sing of your great glory
in this, their joyful hymn of praise:

Holy . . .

Common of Pastors 8: for Several Pastors

This text is substantially the same as that for the Vigil of the Ordination of Saint Ambrose, 7 December.

Common of Doctors of the Church 1

A burning and shining light of teaching, by the gift of the Holy Spirit.

It is truly right and just, our duty and our salvation,
always, here and everywhere to give you thanks,
Lord, holy Father, almighty and eternal God,
through Jesus Christ our Lord.

Christ named his Church
the salt of the earth and light of the world;
a city set on a hilltop, unable to be hidden.
Here Saint N. became illustrious
by the gifts of the Holy Spirit of Christ;
for Christ set *him* as a burning and a shining light
which all might welcome as your gift,
and lift their voice in praise of your great glory.

By word and act we desire to thank you,
as now, united with the choirs of angels
we sing the ageless hymn of your praise:

Holy . . .

Common of Doctors of the Church 2

A teaching of truth, a pure and wholesome harvest, to contradict
error.

It is truly right and just, our duty and our salvation,
always, here and everywhere to give you thanks,
Lord, holy Father, almighty and eternal God.

In your provident care for us you set apart Saint N.
to shed the light of your Gospel
on the hearts and minds of nations.
You set *him* to burn away
what the enemy had sowed amid your harvest
and secure for the storehouse of your Church
the pure and wholesome wheat of catholic teaching.

Yours, Lord God, is the power and grace
which heaven and earth, angels and archangels bless
and all the saints proclaim with ceaseless praise;

Holy . . .

Common of Doctors of the Church 3

Contemplating the word and sharing the fruits of contemplation.

It is truly right and just, our duty and our salvation,
always, here and everywhere to give you thanks,
Lord, holy Father, almighty and eternal God,
through Jesus Christ our Lord.

Christ sowed the word among us
as the seed of a rich harvest
in the lives of those who believe.
Night and day, Saint N. meditated on your word
and from the fruit of contemplation
drew *his* teaching of your truth.
In that same word
he found the unfailing source of wisdom
to lead a life of holiness
and instruct your Church in the doctrine of salvation.

Now, as we celebrate *his* memory
we join the host of angels and saints
in their exultant hymn of praise:

Holy . . .

Common of Virgins 1

*This preface is the same as that for a Virgin Martyr, no. 5 in
the Common of Martyrs.*

Common of Virgins 2

*Christ stands and knocks (cf. Apocalypse 3:20); the Bridegroom
is welcomed with lighted lamps (cf. Matthew 25:1–13).*

It is truly right and just, our duty and our salvation,
always, here and everywhere to give you thanks,
Lord, holy Father, almighty and eternal God,
through Jesus Christ our Lord.

Christ spoke to the heart of your virgin, Saint N.,
and was received by her as a welcome guest,
a beloved bridegroom espoused in steadfast faith.
Father, in this way do your wise virgins
prepare themselves and stand with lamps alight,
keeping watch with longing for Christ your Son,
their greatest and highest desire and love.

Accompanying Christ, they praise him,
who is one with you and the Holy Spirit,
the glory of angels with whom we are united
in this, their ageless hymn of praise:

Holy . . .

Common of Virgins 3

A witness in this present age to that which is to come.

It is truly right and just, our duty and our salvation,
always, here and everywhere to give you thanks,
Lord, holy Father, almighty and eternal God.

You teach us not to rely on this passing life;
you urge us to live in this present brief age
with a heart set on the age that is to come.
Your holy Virgin Saint N. put her faith and hope
in the words of Christ and in his resurrection,
committing herself to him for ever
as a witness to your love.
In her dedication to Christ
she received the gift of a joy beyond words,
being united to him as his own for ever.

Rejoicing in the gift you have given her
we offer praise together with saints and angels
in this, the ageless hymn of your glory:

Holy . . .

Common of Men and Women Saints 1:
a Holy Man (a)

An unmarried saint.

It is truly right and just, our duty and our salvation,
always, here and everywhere to give you thanks,
Lord, holy Father, almighty and eternal God,
through Jesus Christ our Lord.

In the life and witness of your saints
you make your Church rich with new strength
and offer us the faithful pledges of your love.
To fulfil the mystery of our salvation
you give us their example to inspire us
and commend us to their loving intercession.

With joy we call to mind the memory of Saint N.,
who served you with wholehearted loyalty
and now in your glory rejoices for ever.

And so, with him and all your saints
we join to sing of your great glory
in this, their joyful hymn of praise:

Holy . . .

Common of Men and Women Saints 1:
a Holy Man (b)

For the married man, Christ's love is a model for the love between
husband and wife.

It is truly right and just, our duty and our salvation,
always, here and everywhere to give you thanks,
Lord, holy Father, almighty and eternal God,
through Jesus Christ our Lord.

In his great love for the Church,
Christ gave himself to death for her sake
and by this divine example of redemption
he has created a new pattern
for the bond of unity between husband and wife.
With generous heart,
Saint N. took up the vocation of married life
and followed it with a devoted faith.
He made it a means to Christian perfection
so that where he led, others might follow
in walking this way of salvation.

Now he rejoices in you, who called him
and praises you for ever with the powers of heaven,
with whom we also lift our voices
in this, their ageless hymn of praise:

Holy . . .

Common of Men and Women Saints 2:
a Holy Man (c)

A witness to the city which is to come.

It is truly right and just, our duty and our salvation,
always, here and everywhere to give you thanks,
Lord, holy Father, almighty and eternal God.

It is your providence and purpose
to form your saints in the likeness of Christ
and manifest clearly in them
your presence and your likeness.
As we contemplate the life and witness of Saint N.,
you call us to seek more earnestly
your city that is to come,
and we behold in them the trusted way
that leads to blessed union with Christ.

Now, as we celebrate *his* memory
we join the host of angels and saints
in their exultant hymn of praise:

Holy . . .

Common of Men and Women Saints 3: Religious

This preface is used more than once in the Ambrosian Missal. It is found as the Preface for Religious Profession, as well as for the feasts of certain saints such as Ignatius Loyola (in part) and Aloysius Gonzaga. In the Roman Sacramentary it is the Preface for the Rite of Religious Profession.

It is truly right and just, our duty and our salvation,
always, here and everywhere to give you thanks,
Lord, holy Father, almighty and eternal God,
through Jesus Christ our Lord.

Born without sin, as the flower of the Virgin's root,
Christ preached virginity for the kingdom of heaven
and by his living, taught the excellence of chastity.
He chose to follow your will in all things,
and for our sake became obedient even to death,
offering himself to you as the full and acceptable sacrifice.
He consecrated to the service of your glory
those who leave the world to seek you;
and promised them a treasure in heaven.

And so, with them and all the angels and saints
we celebrate your glory
in this, their exultant hymn of praise:

Holy . . .

Common of Men and Women Saints 4: Religious

*The saints recall to us the innocence of our first beginning and
the blessedness of our final goal in heaven.*

It is truly right and just, our duty and our salvation,
always, here and everywhere to give you thanks,
Lord, holy Father, almighty and eternal God.

We celebrate your provident care
as we honour the saints,
who consecrated themselves to Christ
in lives of faith and self-denial
to seek the kingdom of heaven.
Through them, you call the human race
back to the holiness of its first beginning
and invite us to experience the wonderful gifts
that you have prepared for the age to come.

And so, with them and all the angels and saints
we proclaim your glory
in their exultant hymn of praise:

Holy . . .

Common of Men and Women Saints 5:
Saints who Practised Works of Mercy

The great goodness of God to all men and women is mirrored in the saints.

It is truly right and just, our duty and our salvation,
always, here and everywhere to give you thanks,
Lord, holy Father, almighty and eternal God.

You cause the sun to rise on good and bad alike
with one abundant radiance;
you make your rain to fall
on just and unjust in equal measure.
You, Lord God, rewarded your servant Saint N.,
whom your untiring love had made to resemble you.
You opened to *him* the gate of your kingdom,
prepared before the world was made
for those who saw and served Christ
in the poor and in little children.

Now, as we celebrate *his* memory
we join the host of angels and saints
in their exultant hymn of praise:

Holy . . .

Common of Men and Women Saints 6: an Educator

The formation of the young in the likeness of Christ – a pattern for Christian educators to follow.

It is truly right and just, our duty and our salvation,
always, here and everywhere to give you thanks,
Lord, holy Father, almighty and eternal God,
through Jesus Christ our Lord.

Christ showed a special love for little children,
naming them as heirs of the kingdom of heaven.
You desire that such a love be strong in your Church;
and so you endow parents with skills
to bring up their children in wholehearted goodness.
You show how dear to you are those who help the young
to grow to maturity in the likeness of Christ.

And so, in this memorial of Saint N.,
we celebrate your glory,
as with the court of heaven we sing your praise:

Holy . . .

Common of Men and Women Saints 7: for a Holy Woman

Preface identical with that of a male saint.

Common of Men and Women Saints 8: for a Holy Woman

Preface 8a is the same as that for a male saint. Preface 8b is for widows.

It is truly right and just, our duty and our salvation,
always, here and everywhere to give you thanks,
Lord, holy Father, almighty and eternal God,
through Jesus Christ our Lord.

He heard the prayer of widows
and praised their example,
desiring that they be part of that little flock
on whom you, Father, have bestowed the kingdom.
By her gift of simplicity and lowliness of heart,
Saint N. found joy from the Holy Spirit,
by diligent service of her brothers and sisters
in the beloved company of Christ.

Through Christ the choirs of angels
worship forever with joy before your majesty;
with them, we pray you, join our voices
in this, their hymn of joyful supplication:

Holy . . .

Common of Men and Women Saints 9, 10: Several Saints

These two prefaces are identical, and found also in the Roman Sacramentary. The text is based largely on Hebrews 12:1.

It is truly right and just, our duty and our salvation,
always, here and everywhere to give you thanks,
Lord, holy Father, almighty and eternal God.

You are glorified in the assembly of the saints
and by crowning their merits you crown your own gifts.
You give us the example of their life and witness;
you make us one in fellowship with them
and protect us through their constant prayer.
And so, strengthened by such a cloud of witnesses
we can run to victory the race that is before us
and receive with them an inheritance of glory
that will never fade away.

To this destiny Saint N. and Saint N. have come,
whose merits today adorn the heavens.
There, with the choirs of angels and saints
we and they together sing the exultant hymn of praise:

Holy . . .

RITUAL MASSES

For these masses associated with the celebration of the sacraments, the Ambrosian Missal provides prefaces which summarize the rite in question. On some occasions the preface repeats one from another part of the Missal.

The first section covers the Rites of Christian Initiation. Those familiar with the Rite of Christian Initiation of Adults in the Roman Rite will recognize the first two sections dealing with the 'Election' of candidates for Baptism and the 'Scrutinies' held (usually during Lent) to inaugurate their time of close preparation for Baptism, Confirmation and Eucharist.

1. For the Rite of Election

The preface for this rite is that of Saturday 4 of Lent.

2. The Three Scrutinies

The preface is that of Saturday 1 of Lent.

3. For Baptism, i and ii

This rite (for Baptism at other times than at Easter) uses the preface for Wednesday in the Easter Octave 'For the Baptized'.

4. At the Celebration of Confirmation, i

This preface is that of Monday 7 of Eastertide, with a further sentence added for the Confirmation Liturgy.

It is truly right and just, our duty and our salvation,
always, here and everywhere to give you thanks,
Lord, holy Father, almighty and eternal God,
through Jesus Christ our Lord.

Ascending in glory above the highest heaven
and seated at your right hand in power and majesty,
Christ poured out the promised Holy Spirit
on those you had adopted as your children.
Today, on these your servants
this precious gift is bestowed,
to renew their faith in Christ your Son,
and increase in them the gift of holiness
by which their lives may give you glory.

And so, with all the choirs of angels,
we praise your glory, now and for ever,
as with one voice we sing:

Holy . . .

4. At the Celebration of Confirmation, ii

The Acts of the Apostles recalls how the apostles gathered in constant prayer with Mary, the Lord's Mother (cf. Acts 1:12–14). As with the previous preface, this text understands Confirmation as a renewal of the Pentecost event.

It is truly right and just, our duty and our salvation,
always, here and everywhere to give you thanks,
Lord, holy Father, almighty and eternal God.

Through Christ your Son,
enthroned in glory at your right hand
you poured out the promised Holy Spirit
upon the apostles, gathered with Mary the Virgin,
so that they might tell the whole creation
of the wonderful work you have accomplished.
Today, through our saving ministry
you still renew that gift of the Spirit
and continue the great mystery of Pentecost.

And so, with all the choirs of angels,
we praise your glory, now and for ever,
as with one voice we sing:

Holy . . .

5. First Holy Communion of Children

The practice of admitting children to communion at or about the age of seven years dates back to the liturgical reforms of Pope Saint Pius X.

It is truly right and just, our duty and our salvation,
always, here and everywhere to give you thanks,
Lord, holy Father, almighty and eternal God,
through Jesus Christ our Lord.

As the living bread he comes down from heaven
and calls these children to share
the solemn festival of his Passover meal,
admitting them to full communion
in his sacred mysteries.
As today they receive your gift
of sharing in the sacrifice of your Son
they are made one with him in a bond of faith
that they may display more clearly to the world
the holy sacrament that is his Church.

And so, Lord God, with angels and all saints
we exult and glorify your holy name:

Holy . . .

6. The Anointing of the Sick

The Rite of Anointing recalls both Christ's healing power and his sending out of disciples to heal, together with the directions for ministry to the sick in the Letter of Saint James (cf. Mark 6:13; James 5:14).

It is truly right and just, our duty and our salvation,
always, here and everywhere to give you thanks,
Lord, holy Father, almighty and eternal God,
through Jesus Christ our Lord.

By anointing the eyes of the blind
and touching the bodies of the sick
Christ showed his authority over all things
and his loving care for every human sorrow.
He sent his disciples into the world
to take away the afflictions of heart and mind
and to heal the sick through the laying-on of hands.

Recalling these signs of mercy and grace,
given by your Son to bring us deliverance,
we join with all the powers of heaven
to glorify you, the Father,
in their unceasing hymn of praise:

Holy . . .

7. For the Giving of Viaticum and 8.*

As Catholic Christians prepare to die, they are encouraged to receive the sacrament of the body and blood of Christ wherever possible. 'Viaticum' may be translated as 'Food for the Journey'. This preface speaks of Holy Communion as that food, a promise of the eternal banquet of heaven.

It is truly right and just, our duty and our salvation,
always, here and everywhere to give you thanks,
Lord, holy Father, almighty and eternal God.

You fed your people on their desert pilgrimage
with manna sent from heaven,
yet you spared not their lives from death;
for you desired to give us Christ alone
as the true living bread and food of undying life.
Christ has given himself as nourishment for the journey
which leads us to meet you face to face;
and so he has become for us
our consolation amid the sorrows of this age,
the holy pledge of the eternal banquet
and the seed of a glory that will never end.

As we await in faith and joy
the return of the Lord Jesus Christ
we praise you with the angels and saints
in the ceaseless hymn of your glory:

Holy . . .

* There are two masses for The Giving of Viaticum, the second of which has no preface.

9.1 Masses for Husband and Wife, i: Marriage

The three prefaces for a marriage liturgy are found also in the Roman Missal. The first of them is a thanksgiving for the bond of love that increases both the human family and the Church.

It is truly right and just, our duty and our salvation,
always, here and everywhere to give you thanks,
Lord, holy Father, almighty and eternal God.

In the Covenant of marriage
you bring together man and woman
in a gentle but unbroken bond
of harmony and peace;
so that their chaste and fruitful love
may conceive and bear the children
whom you will call to be your own.
By your providence, Lord God,
and by the wonderful workings of your grace,
those same children who will enrich your world
will bring increase also to your Church
through the new birth of baptism.

Through Christ we give you glory
in union with the powers of heaven
in their exultant hymn of praise:

Holy . . .

9.2 Masses for Husband and Wife, i: Marriage

The covenant of marriage is the sacramental way by which God extends to us the plan of salvation.

It is truly right and just, our duty and our salvation,
always, here and everywhere to give you thanks,
Lord, holy Father, almighty and eternal God,
through Jesus Christ our Lord.

You have made a new Covenant with your people,
redeeming them by the death and resurrection of Christ
and making them partakers of your divine nature,
joint heirs with Christ to your eternal glory.
In the bond joining husband and wife
you have expressed this gift of tenderness and grace,
so that the sacrament of marriage
may bind us once again to your love and wisdom.

Therefore with angels and saints
we sing the unceasing hymn of your glory:

Holy . . .

9.3 Masses for Husband and Wife, i: Marriage

Marriage is the way of love towards eternal love, since it is a sacrament of Love itself. The difficulty for a translator here is that Latin has several words for 'love'. English is more limited.

This third marriage preface also appears in each of the three sets of masses to mark wedding anniversaries in the Ambrosian Missal.

It is truly right and just, our duty and our salvation,
always, here and everywhere to give you thanks,
Lord, holy Father, almighty and eternal God.

By your loving act you fashioned man and woman,
bestowing on them such an exalted calling
that in the communion of husband and wife
you show us the true image of your love.
From that same love you created us,
and in your law of love you bid us walk;
until you make us partakers
of that love which has no end.
The holy sacrament of marriage
stands as a sign of your tenderness towards us,
and as the wonderful consecration of all human love,
through Jesus Christ our Lord.

Through Christ we give you glory
with angels and heavenly powers
in their exultant hymn of praise:

Holy . . .

10. The Blessing of an Abbot or Abbess

The preface is the same as that in the Common of Saints 3: Religious.

11. The Consecration of Virgins, i

Consecrated virginity takes as its model the virginal conception of Christ. The last four lines are more a paraphrase than a translation, in order to clarify the sequence of thought.

It is truly right and just, our duty and our salvation,
always, here and everywhere to give you thanks,
Lord, holy Father, almighty and eternal God,
through Jesus Christ our Lord.

He came upon earth to restore what we had lost,
and for his conception in human flesh
he consecrated the womb of the Virgin
to be his earthly dwelling place,
making her the temple of God
and shrine of purest innocence.
Today we rejoice in this new consecration
bestowed by the Holy Spirit;
a call to bear fruit in virginity
and extend to us the work of salvation
revealed to us by Christ, your Son, our Lord.

With Christ your whole Church gives praise
as she sees her children commit their lives
to your eternal and loving purposes;
and so with the choirs of angels we sing your praise:

Holy . . .

11. The Consecration of Virgins, ii

12. First Religious Profession; Perpetual Profession, i and ii; Renewal of Vows; Anniversary of Profession

For these masses the preface is that in the Common of Saints 3: Religious.

13. i The Day of Dedication of a Church

Two prefaces are given for this day, the first for the Rite of Dedication itself.

Eternal Father, it is truly right and just
that we should always give you thanks and praise.

You created the whole universe as your temple,
so that in every place your name might be glorified;
yet you do not refuse the hallowing
of places prepared for the celebration of your mysteries.
And so with joy we dedicate
this house of prayer, built by human hands.
Here is foreshadowed the true temple which is Christ,
and the image of the heavenly Jerusalem.
You consecrated the body of your Son, born of the Virgin,
to be the holy dwelling place
where your Godhead abides in its fullness.
You established your Church as the holy city
securely founded and built upon the apostles
with Jesus Christ himself the cornerstone.

You build it with chosen stones
given life by the Spirit and bonded together in love.
In this city you will be all in all, for endless ages,
and Christ will shine as its eternal light.

Through him we give you thanks, Lord God,
in union with angels and all the powers of heaven
in their exultant hymn of praise:

Holy . . .

13. ii The Day of Dedication of a Church

The second preface is for use on the day of dedication at other masses.

It is truly right and just, our duty and our salvation,
always, here and everywhere to give you thanks,
Lord, holy Father, almighty and eternal God.

Today you have consecrated this house
to embrace our prayer and acts of worship,
in the sacred rites which bring us salvation.
The beauty of this house
foretells the glory of your whole Church,
adorned with signs of your saving power
and lifted up from earth to heaven.
The Church is the fruitful mother of all who live,
the sacrament of life and salvation for all believers.
Your Church is the bride of Christ the Lamb,
clothed with his radiance;
for her sake he bore the cross and overcame our enemy.
Standing now at your right hand in the heavenly places
and bright with the faith and good works of her children
she invokes the majesty of your Godhead
in the threefold hymn of praise.

Your Church on earth unites with your Church above
and with the choirs of angels
in that same hymn of exultation:

Holy . . .

13. iii The Dedication of an Altar

Christ sums up in himself the types of worship from the Old
Covenant and embodies the true worship: lives dedicated like his
to God.

It is truly right and just, our duty and our salvation,
always, here and everywhere to give you thanks,
Lord, holy Father, almighty and eternal God,
through Jesus Christ our Lord.

He is the true priest and the true saving victim
who offered himself to you on the altar of the cross
and commanded us to celebrate
the memorial of that sacrifice for ever.
And so your people have built this altar
which we dedicate to you, Lord God, in joy and praise.
This is a true place of worship
where the sacrifice of Christ
is enacted in a holy mystery;
where perfect praise is given to you
and our redemption is made manifest.
Here is prepared the Lord's table
where your children are strengthened by the body of Christ
and gathered into the one holy Church.
Here your people may drink of the Spirit
in waters flowing from Christ the spiritual rock;
through him they will become
a holy offering and a living altar.

Therefore, Lord God, with the angels and powers of heaven
we exult and glorify your holy name:

Holy . . .

MASSES FOR VARIOUS NEEDS

This collection of masses is intended to provide texts for celebrations of Church and civil events and intentions.

1.1 For the Holy Church: The Universal Church, i

This preface uses text from the preface of the Mass for the dedication anniversary, in the dedicated church.

It is truly right and just, our duty and our salvation,
always, here and everywhere to give you thanks,
Lord, holy Father, almighty and eternal God.

You are the steadfast builder of a temple,
which is ourselves, your people.
You make your Church throughout the world
grow into the one body of Christ our Lord,
to reach its fullness in the vision of peace
that is the heavenly city, the new Jerusalem.

Therefore with angels and saints
we sing the unceasing hymn of your glory:

Holy . . .

1.2 For the Holy Church: The Universal Church, ii

The Church is celebrated as Bride and Mother, bound to Christ and rejoicing in those newly initiated through the 'new birth' of Baptism, Confirmation and Eucharist.

It is truly right and just, our duty and our salvation,
always, here and everywhere to give you thanks,
Lord, holy Father, almighty and eternal God.

By the working of the Holy Spirit
you hallow the Church, the Bride of Christ,
so that as the joyful mother of many children
she may be given a place amid your glory
in the kingdom of heaven.

Therefore with angels and saints
we sing the unceasing hymn of your glory:

Holy . . .

1.3 For the Church: The Universal Church, iii

This preface is taken from the body of the Missal, Sunday 15 of Ordinary Time.

1.4 For the Church: The Universal Church, iv

This text is found also in the Roman Sacramentary, where it is the Preface for Christian Unity.

It is truly right and just, our duty and our salvation,
always, here and everywhere to give you thanks,
Lord, holy Father, almighty and eternal God,
through Jesus Christ our Lord.

Through Christ you have brought us
to the knowledge of your truth,
so that we might become his body,
bound together by one faith and one baptism.
Through Christ you have bestowed your Holy Spirit
on all the peoples of the earth.
From a rich diversity of gifts
the Spirit creates a wonderful unity,
dwelling in the hearts of your adopted children,
filling the whole Church and guiding it in wisdom.

And so, with all the choirs of angels,
we praise your glory, now and for ever,
as with one voice we sing:

Holy . . .

2. For the Church: The Local Church

This text reflects the Second Vatican Council's teaching that each local church makes manifest and real the mystery of the Church Universal.

It is truly right and just, our duty and our salvation,
always, here and everywhere to give you thanks,
Lord, holy Father, almighty and eternal God.

You sustain this beloved portion of your people
with constant gifts of grace,
so that in fellowship with our Bishop
we may experience a communion of faith and love
with your whole Church throughout the world.
In this way, enriched by the gifts of your Holy Spirit,
the Church will make effective here on earth
the mystery of Christ's abiding presence
and the salvation he came to bring.

And so, with all the choirs of angels,
we praise your glory, now and for ever,
as with one voice we sing:

Holy . . .

3. For the Church: The Pope

Preface from the feast of Saint Peter's Chair in the Proper of Saints, 22 February.

4. For the Church: The Bishop (Anniversary of Ordination)

Preface from the Mass of Chrism in Holy Week.

5. For the Church: Election of Pope or Bishop

Two prefaces for this occasion, the first from the feast of Saint Peter's Chair, 22 February; the second from the Mass of Chrism in Holy Week.

6. For the Church: A Council or Synod

The Preface for Sunday 15 of Ordinary Time is used.

7. For the Church: For Priests

The Preface for the Mass of Chrism in Holy Week is used.

8. For the Church: For Vocations to Holy Orders

It is truly right and just, our duty and our salvation,
always, here and everywhere to give you thanks,
Lord, holy Father, almighty and eternal God,
through Jesus Christ your beloved Son.

Christ bids us ask the Lord of the harvest
to send labourers into his vineyard,
so that as the Church journeys on its pilgrimage
there will always be those
who will break the bread of his saving word
for those little ones who seek it
and bring the gifts of redemption
to all in any kind of need.

Therefore with angels and saints
we sing the unceasing hymn of your glory:

Holy . . .

9. For the Church: For Religious

The Preface of Religious Profession is used.

10. For the Church: For Vocations to the Religious Life

The Preface for Religious Profession is used.

11. For the Church: For Apostolic Activity

The Preface of Sunday 7 of Ordinary Time is used.

12. For the Church: For Christian Education

The true purpose of education: to mature in the love and grace of Christ.

It is truly right and just, our duty and our salvation,
always, here and everywhere to give you thanks,
Lord, holy Father, almighty and eternal God,
through Jesus Christ our Lord.

You created us in the likeness of Christ
who is the perfect example of human living.
In Christ we find our destiny,
our release from the bonds of evil
and our maturity in love and grace.
In this way, you will accomplish in us
the mystery of your call to fullness of life.

Your Son became incarnate, the child of a human family;
he offers himself as the pattern
by which children may be brought up
to grow like him in wisdom
and in your gracious favour.

Therefore with angels and saints
we sing the unceasing hymn of your glory:

Holy . . .

13. For the Church: Young People–Profession of Faith

Vocation, encounter, friendship, mission. These are the themes of this celebration of growing Christian faith.

It is truly right and just, our duty and our salvation,
always, here and everywhere to thank you,
the all-holy and generous Father,
for all that you have given to us
and in your loving mercy continue to bestow.

With a father's love you have brought us to life
and called each one of us by name,
assigning to us our own unique vocation.
You sent your only Son to be our Saviour,
to seek us out and meet us on our way
and form with each of us
a bond of steadfast friendship.
You call us to be co-workers with Christ
in his ministry of salvation;
you make us members of his Church,
to share its mission of working for peace
and announcing your good news to the world.

And so, with heaven's angels and saints,
and those who seek your justice here on earth,
we sing the ageless hymn of your glory:

Holy . . .

14. For the Church: Christian Old Age

Life as a preparation for the life to come.

It is truly right and just, our duty and our salvation,
always, here and everywhere to give you thanks,
Lord, holy Father, almighty and eternal God,
through Jesus Christ our Lord.

You give us length of days as a token of your love,
and as they pass you teach us to take delight
in that life which will endure for all eternity.
You accompany our journey
with the many gifts of Christ,
that we may remain in your love as our years increase
and fulfil the purpose to which you call us.
Though bodily vigour may fade,
your ceaseless love is always new;
for you strengthen in us the gifts of your Spirit
that we may make our way, secure in hope,
to you, the Lord in whom we put our faith.

For all your gifts we give you praise,
and looking forward to a joy that has no end
we join the exultant powers of heaven
in this, their ceaseless hymn of praise:

Holy . . .

15. For the Church: For the Unity of Christians

The preface from the Mass for the Church, 4, is used.

16. For the Church: For the Evangelization of Peoples

The preface from the Mass for the Church, 11, is used.

17. For the Church: For Persecuted Christians

The preface for the Wednesday in Holy Week is used.

18. For the Church: Pastoral or Spiritual Meetings

A preface celebrating the gift of the Holy Spirit.

It is truly right and just, our duty and our salvation,
always, here and everywhere to give you thanks,
Lord, holy Father, almighty and eternal God,
through Jesus Christ our Lord.

Having accomplished the work you gave him to do,
Christ our Lord sent the Holy Spirit
to rule and teach the Church,
that all who believe may come to know you
and share in the mystery of salvation.

And so, with the all the powers of heaven
we on earth acclaim your glory
in this, our ageless hymn of praise:

Holy . . .

19. For the Church: Spiritual Exercises

Seeking God, listening in faith, conformed to Christ.

It is truly right and just, our duty and our salvation,
always, here and everywhere to give you thanks,
Lord, holy Father, almighty and eternal God.

You call us together to listen in faith
to the voice of your Holy Spirit,
so that our lives may be open
to the promptings of your grace
and conformed more closely to Christ your Son.
In Christ you chose us before all ages,
intending us to follow your way of faith,
to be filled with your hope and renewed in your love.

As we seek you, the source and summit of holiness,
we trust in your strength to come to our aid,
as with angels we sing the unceasing hymn of praise:

Holy . . .

20.1 For the Church: Priests' Meetings/Retreats, i

A text reflecting on the ministry of presbyters in union with Christ.

It is truly right and just, our duty and our salvation,
always, here and everywhere to give you thanks,
Lord, holy Father, almighty and eternal God.

Through the ministry of the Bishop
who ordains and sends them to share his mission,
you consecrate priests to serve Christ
our king and priest and teacher.
You call them to share in his work of salvation,
so that as he died and rose again
and by his Spirit created the Church,
so also his Church may grow throughout the world
and be joyfully manifest as the people of God,
the body of Christ and the living temple of the Spirit.

As we celebrate the abundance of your gifts,
we glorify you with the service of our praise
as with angels and saints we glorify your name:

Holy . . .

20.2 For the Church: Priests' Meetings/Retreats, ii

A text reflecting on the ministry of presbyters as ministers of salvation in communion with the Bishop.

It is truly right and just, our duty and our salvation,
always, here and everywhere to give you thanks,
Lord, holy Father, almighty and eternal God,
through Jesus Christ our Lord.

He is your Word who feeds and sustains your people;
the source of that gracious compassion
which seeks out sinners and calls them to conversion.
Moved by the Spirit, he chose apostles,
so that the work of your mercy
accomplished in his death and resurrection
might be effective throughout our earthly pilgrimage.
In that same Spirit
he ordains bishops and gives them their mission
to be shared with presbyters,
their co-workers in the priesthood,
so that in a joyful and fraternal communion
they may minister to us his word and sacraments.

We praise you for these great gifts to your Church
and with all who stand before the altar of the Lamb
we sing the unceasing hymn of your praise:

Holy . . .

20.3 For the Church: Priests' Meetings/Retreats, iii

The preface for the first of these three masses is used.

21.1 For Public Needs: For Peace

This preface weaves together five New Testament texts: Apocalypse 21:5; John 1:16; Philippians 2:6–9; Colossians 1:19–20 and Hebrews 5:9.

It is truly right and just, our duty and our salvation,
always, here and everywhere to give you thanks,
Lord, holy Father, almighty and eternal God,
through Jesus Christ our Lord.

In Christ you have made all things new
and given us all a share in his fullness.
Though he was in the form of God,
he emptied himself
and by shedding his blood on the cross
he brought peace for the whole creation.
Therefore he was exalted above all things,
being made the source of eternal salvation
for all who serve him.

And so, with all the powers of heaven
we glorify your name
in their unceasing hymn of praise:

Holy . . .

21.2 For Public Needs: For Justice

Justice is fulfilled by keeping the command to love as Christ has loved us.

It is truly right and just, our duty and our salvation,
always, here and everywhere to give you thanks,
Lord, holy Father, almighty and eternal God,
through Jesus Christ our Lord.

Through Christ you have created us
and with boundless love redeemed us,
adopting us as your children
and filling us with the gifts of your Spirit.
You bid us love each other as you love us,
to imitate Jesus who gave himself for us
and work boldly for the justice he revealed.
You call us to break with selfish desires
and share with a cheerful heart
what you have generously given for all.
You urge us to work for peace and justice,
and so prepare the way of the heavenly kingdom.

In hope of this kingdom we praise your name,
as with angels and saints we sing in joy
the hymn of your glory and praise:

Holy . . .

21.3 For Public Needs: For Liberty

Freedom is the right of the children of God.

It is truly right and just, our duty and our salvation,
always, here and everywhere to give you thanks,
Lord, holy Father, almighty and eternal God.

You created men and women in dignity and honour,
and through Christ your Son
you gave them the great gift of freedom.
You implant in them the desire for true liberty,
which is their dignity as your children
and the right of every people.
Father and Redeemer of all, you call us
not to slavery, which mars the beauty of your work,
but to a wise exercise of our free will,
by which we come to resemble you.
You wish us to grow in the freedom of Christ
and reach that perfection in him
which you have willed and purposed
from the foundation of the world.

Therefore with angels and saints
we sing the unceasing hymn of your glory:

Holy . . .

21.4 For Public Needs: In Time of War or Unrest

The preface from the Mass for Peace is said.

21.5 For Public Events: Beginning of the Civil Year

The preface for Sunday 10 of Ordinary Time is used.

21.6 For Public Events: Beginning of the School Year

A preface on the theme of Wisdom.

It is truly right and just, our duty and our salvation,
always, here and everywhere to give you thanks,
Lord, holy Father, almighty and eternal God.

Through the coming of Christ,
your uncreated Wisdom,
you have revealed to us
the knowledge of your holy name
and of your infinite power and glory;
so that, humbly praising your majesty
and faithfully following your commandments,
we may lay hold of that blessed gift
which is eternal life and truth.

And so, throughout the heavens and the earth
all things adore you and sing a new song;
and we with all the angels give you glory
in this, their ever-joyful hymn of praise:

Holy . . .

21.7 For Public Events: The Sanctification of Human Labour

This text dwells upon the sanctification of human work by Jesus as the labourer's Son, while naming the true dignity of human labour as preparing the 'new heaven and new earth'.

It is truly right and just, our duty and our salvation,
always, here and everywhere to give you thanks,
Lord, holy Father, almighty and eternal God,
through Jesus Christ our Lord.

Christ was our Redeemer
even while working with his own hands
in the home at Nazareth;
in this way he gave a new dignity to human labour.
He invites our human work to play its part
in the mystery of salvation
which he has accomplished.
He desires that our endeavours
should complete your plan of creation,
so that as we toil in faith and love
we may know that by your gift we are preparing the way
that leads to your new heaven and new earth.

Therefore with angels and saints
we sing the unceasing hymn of your glory:

Holy . . .

21.8 For Public Events: The Time of Sowing the Fields

The preface for Sunday 10 of Ordinary Time is used.

21.9 For Public Events: After the Harvest

The preface for Sunday 10 of Ordinary Time is used.

21.10 For Public Needs: In Time of Famine or for Those Suffering Hunger

The preface of Monday 4 of Lent is used.

21.11 For Public Needs: For Refugees and Exiles

The preface of Thursday 5 of Lent is used.

21.12 For Public Needs: In Praise of the Creator of All

This lengthy piece reflects on the function of the human race in creation and the final destiny of everything.

Father, it is right to give you thanks
because every day you delight us
with the wonders of your creation,
giving us joy in all that your hands have made.
In Christ, the firstborn and pattern of that creation,
your all-powerful Word formed everything out of nothing
and entrusted this world to humankind,
to men and women fashioned in your likeness
as the bearers of your glory.
From you, most high, most loving and all-wise,
our race received the earth to be its home.
You willed that we should be earth's careful stewards,
transforming it and making it fruitful
according to your command,
so that it might bring forth food for the body
and light for the spirit
to the grateful praise of your holy name.

You have raised all of creation to new dignity
through your Son, incarnate for us in human flesh.
By your mysterious providence
you endow every part of it with that Holy Spirit
who delivers from evil and the slavery of sin.
Father, in this great gift of love,
everything that you named as good from the beginning
now awaits the revelation of your sons and daughters
and the appearing of new heavens and earth.
Here, everything is to be made new,
the corruption of death destroyed,

and humankind, risen to new life in Christ,
shall come to make its dwelling.

Through Christ,
the angels and saints together give you glory.
With them we join our voice in joy and praise:

Holy . . .

21.13 For Public Needs: For the Sick

Sickness and pain are hallowed by the Passion of Christ.

It is truly right and just, our duty and our salvation,
always, here and everywhere to give you thanks,
Lord, holy Father, almighty and eternal God,
through Jesus Christ our Lord.

In deepest love for us he bore his passion,
calling us to follow him as our example
and showing us the path of light and salvation.
In this way he desired us to enter more deeply
into the mystery of his suffering and death,
so that he might hallow our pain
and prepare us for the glory that is to come.
By healing our infirmities and sickness
he announced the advent of your rule.
He offered the torments of his death
to purchase our freedom from evil;
he desired that the way of the cross
should be the way that leads to your glory.

Through Christ therefore, we give you praise,
as we join angels and saints
in their unceasing hymn of praise:

Holy . . .

21.14 For Public Needs: For the Dying

The preface of the previous Mass for the Sick is used.

21.15 For Public Needs: In Any Necessity

The preface for Wednesday 4 of Lent is used.

21.16 For Public Needs: In Thanksgiving

The preface for Wednesday 4 of Lent is used.

22.1 For Individual Needs:
For the Forgiveness of Sins, i

The preface for Thursday 2 of Lent is used.

22.2 For Individual Needs: For the Forgiveness of Sins, ii

The preface for Tuesday 3 of Lent is used.

22.3 For Individual Needs: To Pray for Charity, i

All of one mind in the love of Christ.

It is truly right and just, our duty and our salvation,
always, here and everywhere to give you thanks,
Lord, holy Father, almighty and eternal God.

You draw your people together in mutual love
and bind them to yourself in a covenant of peace.
You command that no-one should do to another
what they would not have done to themselves.
You bid us to share those good things
which nature desires for self alone.
Thus, while each of us seeks their true self
in love of their neighbour,
all may be of one mind in the love of Christ.

Therefore with angels and saints
we sing the unceasing hymn of your glory:

Holy . . .

22.4 For Individual Needs: To Pray for Charity, ii

The preface for Sunday 3 of Lent is used.

22.5 For Individual Needs: For Concord

The preface for Sunday 6 of Ordinary Time is used.

22.6 For Individual Needs: For the Family

The preface of the feast of the Holy Family is used.

22.7 For Individual Needs: To Pray for the Grace of Dying Well

The preface from Masses for the Dead 6 is used.

VOTIVE MASSES

Votive masses are devotional liturgies celebrated for special occasions (and sometimes on certain days of the week) in honour of God or the Mystery of Salvation or major saints.

1. Of the Holy Trinity

The preface for Trinity Sunday is used.

2. Of the Mystery of the Holy Cross, i

The preface for the feast of the Exaltation of the Holy Cross is used.

2. Of the Mystery of the Holy Cross, ii

This preface is found also in the Roman Missal as the preface for the feast of the Exaltation of the Cross.

It is truly right and just, our duty and our salvation,
always, here and everywhere to give you thanks,
Lord, holy Father, almighty and eternal God.

You willed that our salvation
should take place on the wood of the cross,
so that where death had its beginning,
there life itself might rise again,

318

and our enemy, who conquered by a tree,
might on a tree be overcome
through Jesus Christ our Lord.

Through Christ the choirs of angels
worship forever with joy before your majesty;
with them, we pray you, join our voices
in this, their hymn of joyful supplication:

Holy . . .

2. Of the Mystery of the Holy Cross, iii

A preface similar in theme to the previous text but with a more developed imagery.

It is truly right and just, our duty and our salvation,
always, here and everywhere to give you thanks,
Lord, holy Father, almighty and eternal God,
through Jesus Christ our Lord.

By suffering death upon the cross
Christ in great mercy redeemed the world.
The tree of the cross brought healing for our fall,
and allayed the bitterness of that other tree,
whose taste brought death into the world.
Now by the powerful sign of the cross
Christ has conquered death,
so that by the triumph of his resurrection
he might lead us back to paradise, our true home.

And so, with all the choirs of angels,
we praise your glory, now and for ever,
as with one voice we sing:

Holy . . .

3. Of the Holy Eucharist i, ii

The preface for the feast of the Body and Blood of Christ is used.

3. Of the Holy Eucharist, iii

The preface for Sunday 2 of Christmas is used, omitting the last line.

4. Of the Holy Name of Jesus

Christ signs his followers with his name, the name which means salvation.

It is truly right and just, our duty and our salvation,
always, here and everywhere to give you thanks,
Lord, holy Father, almighty and eternal God,
through Jesus Christ our Lord.

You sent your only Son to us,
bearing the name that speaks of salvation,
so that he might set us free
from the tyranny of sin, our ancient foe,
and by signing us with his name as your children,
might call us to share the glory of your kingdom.
This is the name of our thanksgiving;
before this name all knees must bend;
this is the name we invoke
as a refuge amid the perils of this life
and a strong support in the hour of death.

We join with all creation to praise his name
as with the choirs of heaven
we sing the ageless hymn of your glory:

Holy . . .

5. The Precious Blood of Jesus Christ our Lord

*The preface for Thursday in the Easter Octave (For the Baptized)
is used.*

6. The Sacred Heart of Jesus, i

The preface for the feast of the Sacred Heart is used.

6. The Sacred Heart of Jesus, ii

Surely he has borne our griefs.

It is truly right and just, our duty and our salvation,
always, here and everywhere to give you thanks,
Lord, holy Father, almighty and eternal God.

You so loved the world that you gave your Son
to bear our griefs and carry our sorrows
and receive the wound of our transgressions.
In the deepest love of his sacred heart
he laid down his life for those who were his enemies
and offered himself as a sacrifice of peace;
that we, who were yet sinners
might in his blood be reconciled to you.

And so, we celebrate the riches of that love
which he pours out unceasingly upon his Church.
We join the angels and the saints
as they stand in the sight of your glory
and praise you without end:

Holy . . .

7. Of the Holy Spirit, i

Source of our sanctification, revealer of Christ.

It is truly right and just, our duty and our salvation,
always, here and everywhere to give you thanks,
Lord, holy Father, almighty and eternal God,
through Jesus Christ our Lord.

Ascending in glory above the highest heaven
and seated at your right hand in power and majesty,
Christ poured out the promised Holy Spirit
upon your adopted children.
You give that same Spirit still to your Church
as the wellspring of all holiness,
revealing the riches of Christ through many gifts
and bringing to us the fruits of your boundless love.

And so, with all the choirs of angels,
we praise your glory, now and for ever,
as with one voice we sing:

Holy . . .

7. Of the Holy Spirit, ii

The Spirit given to the Church.

It is truly right and just, our duty and our salvation,
always, here and everywhere to give you thanks,
Lord, holy Father, almighty and eternal God.

You bestow your gifts for every age and season,
guiding your Church with a wonderful care.
In the power of the Spirit,
sent by your Son,
you never cease to uphold your people,
so that with a heart set on you
they may seek your aid in their troubles
and return thanks to you in all their joys.

Therefore with angels and saints
we sing the unceasing hymn of your glory:

Holy . . .

7. Of the Holy Spirit, iii

The preface for the Votive Mass of the Holy Spirit, i, is used.

8. Of the Blessed Virgin Mary

The prefaces from the Common of the Blessed Virgin Mary are used according to the season.

9. Of the Holy Angels

Ministers of God's love for us.

It is truly right and just, our duty and our salvation,
always, here and everywhere to give you thanks,
Lord, holy Father, almighty and eternal God.

You reveal your wise purpose
for the salvation of the human race
by assigning to the angels
the ministry of your steadfast love.
While they contemplate your splendour,
standing before you and singing your praise,
they keep a faithful vigil for us
along the way that leads to life,
and guide us towards the kingdom of your light.

In joyful gladness we unite our voice with theirs
and sing the ageless hymn of your praise:

Holy . . .

326

10. Of Saint Joseph

The preface for the feast of Saint Joseph is used.

11. Of the Holy Apostles

This preface is found in the Roman Missal as the Preface of Apostles 2.

It is truly right and just, our duty and our salvation,
always, here and everywhere to give you thanks,
Lord, holy Father, almighty and eternal God.

You have built the Church of Christ your Son
upon the foundation of the apostles,
so that it should for ever stand firm
as the sign of your holiness upon earth
and a witness for humankind
to your eternal kingdom of heaven.

And so, with all the choirs of angels,
we praise your glory, now and for ever,
as with one voice we sing:

Holy . . .

12. Of Saint Peter, Apostle

The preface for the Chair of Saint Peter, 22 February, is used.

13. Of Saint Paul, Apostle

The preface for the Conversion of Saint Paul, 25 January, is used.

14. Of One Apostle

The preface for Saint Simon and Saint Jude, 28 October, is used.

15. Of All Saints

The preface for All Saints' Day, 1 November, is used.

MASSES FOR THE DEAD

1. Of One Dead Person, i

Restored through the resurrection of Christ.

It is truly right and just, our duty and our salvation,
always, here and everywhere to give you thanks,
Lord, holy Father, almighty and eternal God.

By your command we are born, by your will we are
    governed
and through your saving work we have been redeemed.
At your bidding, we leave this world
and become as the earth from which we were taken;
yet through Christ we are restored to the glory of
    resurrection.
For our own sins, Lord, we perish,
but you, the source of all compassion,
call us once more to the gift of life with Christ.

And so, with all the powers of heaven,
we on earth rejoice before you
in the ageless hymn of your glory:

Holy . . .

1. Of One Dead Person, ii

The liturgical 'memorial' of salvation is itself a source of hope in eternal life. The ancient Christian expression 'Life is changed, not ended' (from an account of the martyrdom of Saint Symphorian) will be familiar to those who use the Roman Rite.

It is truly right and just, our duty and our salvation,
always, here and everywhere to give you thanks,
Lord, holy Father, almighty and eternal God.
In your kindness you welcome all believers
and bring them to eternal glory in union with Christ.

Though the law of death
has brought sadness to the human heart,
the gift of your mercy arouses in us
the hope of an immortality to come,
while the remembrance of our salvation
dispels all fear of departing from this world.
By your compassion, Lord,
the life of your people is changed, not ended;
and those who have given you honour in this world
will gain in death a home of eternal joy.

In thanksgiving for your loving purposes
we glorify you with angels and saints
in this, their exultant hymn of praise:

Holy . . .

1. Of One Dead Person, iii

This preface celebrates the dying and rising of Christ at the
funeral liturgy. In its use of 1 Corinthians 15:53, the text closes
with a powerful affirmation of the central theme of Christian
dying: 'This perishable body must put on imperishability and
this mortal body must clothe itself with immortality.'

It is truly right and just, our duty and our salvation,
always, here and everywhere to give you thanks,
Lord, holy Father, almighty and eternal God,
through Jesus Christ our Lord.

As the Word made Flesh,
he came to live in lowly form among us.
As the Immortal One, he assumed our mortality
to suffer on the cross and be laid in the tomb.
But with great power he has risen from the dead
so that he might raise us together with himself
and clothe our corruptible nature
with the incorruption of eternal life.

In praise of your wonderful work
and in the hope of your unending bliss,
we join the hosts of angels and saints
in their new song of everlasting praise:

Holy . . .

1. Of One Dead Person, iv

Like the previous text, this preface looks to the dying and rising
of Christ as that which promises freedom from sin and death.

It is truly right and just, our duty and our salvation,
always, here and everywhere to give you thanks,
Lord, holy Father, almighty and eternal God,
through Jesus Christ our Lord.

In fulfilment of your saving purposes
he experienced death, the fruit of sin,
in order to break its bonds and free the human race.
By his great power he rose from the dead,
that he might offer us to you in glory and freedom,
making us heirs with himself to your eternal kingdom.

And so, with the angels and saints who adore you
we sing your glory both now and for eternity:

Holy . . .

1. Of One Dead Person, v

*Christ, the firstborn from the dead, firstfruits of the resurrection
(cf. 1 Corinthians 15:20; Colossians 1:18).*

It is truly right and just, our duty and our salvation,
always, here and everywhere to give you thanks,
Lord, holy Father, almighty and eternal God,
through Jesus Christ our Lord.

He has rescued earthly men and women
from the embrace of death,
revealing to us the wonder of his resurrection.
Christ, the firstborn of those who die,
has shown himself the firstfruits
of those who rise from the dead.
Lord God, by this promise of heaven
you strengthen our faith,
you lift our mind to you, our greatest good;
you lighten all our grief
with your abiding consolation.

Our heart rejoices in your glory
and we share the joy of all your saints
in this, their crown of joy and praise:

Holy . . .

2. Several Dead

'Marked with the sign of faith' in Baptism, Christians can be confident in the sure and certain hope of eternal life.

It is truly right and just, our duty and our salvation,
always, here and everywhere to give you thanks,
Lord, holy Father, almighty and eternal God,
through Jesus Christ our Lord.

By his passion we have been redeemed
and by his resurrection, taken into glorious liberty.
In Christ the power of death is broken
and with him we enter into eternal life.
Your mercy gives us boundless hope
that all who have been marked
with the sign of Christian faith
shall receive from you the forgiveness of sins
and an eternal dwelling in your kingdom of light.

And so, with the choirs of angels and saints
we celebrate your power and glory
in this, their ageless hymn of praise:

Holy . . .

3. Anniversary: One Dead Person, i

We are baptized into the death of Christ (Romans 6:3). Christ,
the Second Adam, restores what the First Adam had lost (cf.
1 Corinthians 15:45–9).

It is truly right and just, our duty and our salvation,
always, here and everywhere to give you thanks,
Lord, holy Father, almighty and eternal God,
through Jesus Christ our Lord.

In the waters of baptism
we were plunged into the death of Christ.
We died for ever to the sin of the First Adam,
so as to rise again into the grace of the Second.
Christ has willed us to share in his life,
to be blessed beyond measure with his immortality
and fulfilled in his presence with unending joy.

And so, with all the choirs of heaven
we acclaim your majesty and glory
in this one song of joyful praise:

Holy . . .

3. Anniversary: One Dead Person, ii

Of those who walked Christ's path of sorrow, Mary his Mother
holds the first place. This text names Mary as an active participant
in the process of mourning for those who have died.

It is truly right and just, our duty and our salvation,
always, here and everywhere to give you thanks,
Lord, holy Father, almighty and eternal God,
through Jesus Christ our Lord.

For us he was made subject to the power of death,
so that all who walk with him in this time of tears
might receive a great weight of glory
through his resurrection from the dead.
In suffering the passion,
he made his Virgin Mother one with himself;
he gave her to us, to become our consolation
amid the sorrows of this life
and the joyful gate of entry
into our true heavenly home.

And so, we join our voice
to the song of angels and saints
who glorify your goodness
in songs of unceasing praise:

Holy . . .

3. Anniversary: One Dead Person, iii

The hope of lasting fellowship with the saints, sharing in the triumph of Christ's resurrection.

It is truly right and just, our duty and our salvation,
always, here and everywhere to give you thanks,
Lord, holy Father, almighty and eternal God.

Amid the griefs and afflictions of death,
you give to those who believe in you
the hope of a lasting fellowship with the saints,
where soul and body are made new in life eternal.
Through the passion of your Son,
you, Lord God, enable us to await in hope
the glory of his resurrection,
that we who are united with him in death
may share in his eternal victory.

Therefore, with all the powers of heaven,
we glorify you joyfully on earth
in this, their ageless hymn of praise:

Holy . . .

4. Anniversary: Several Dead

Christ our life, the resurrection of the dead.

It is truly right and just, our duty and our salvation,
always, here and everywhere to give you thanks,
Lord, holy Father, almighty and eternal God,
through Jesus Christ our Lord.

Christ is the Saviour of the world,
the life of all, the resurrection of the dead.
In love beyond all telling
he came to share our human condition,
to bear our griefs and the burden of our sins;
he came to turn the dread sentence of death
into the gift of eternal life.
By dying and rising, he accomplished our redemption;
securing for us a joyful hope
and lightening the sorrow of our departure from this world.

With heartfelt love we acclaim your gift,
as with the host of heaven we lift our voice in praise:

Holy . . .

5. Various Commemorations, i: One Dead Person

The preceding preface is used.

5. Various Commemorations, ii: One Dead Person

The first of the prefaces for masses of the dead is used.

5. Various Commemorations, iii: One Dead Person

The fourth of the prefaces in this section is used.

6. Various Commemorations, i: For Several People or for All the Dead

The preface from the Anniversary set, ii, is used.

6. Various Commemorations, ii: For Several People or for All the Dead

The Body follows the Head; Christ goes before us into glory.

It is truly right and just, our duty and our salvation,
always, here and everywhere to give you thanks,
Lord, holy Father, almighty and eternal God,
through Jesus Christ our Lord.

He desired that his Virgin Mother and all the saints
should be sharers with him in his passion,
so that where he has gone before, as head of the mystical body,
there also the members, given life by him,
should follow in his glory.
Christ freely gave himself to death
so as to precede his members in resurrection.
As he is the first to enter heaven in triumph,
he gives his members a sure and joyful hope
of inheriting eternal life.

Supported in our mortality by this immortal gift,
we join the angels and saints who contemplate your glory
to sing this song of glory and praise:

Holy . . .

6. Various Commemorations, iii: For Several People or for All the Dead

The preface for the Anniversary of One Dead Person, i, is used.

7. Various Prayers for the Dead – The Pope

With appropriate variations, this preface is also used for commemorations of bishops and priests.

It is truly right and just, our duty and our salvation,
always, here and everywhere to give you thanks,
Lord, holy Father, almighty and eternal God,
through Jesus Christ our Lord.

In his wisdom and mercy we place our trust,
that in the courts of heaven
he will allot a place of honour to those
to whom he committed the governance of his Church.*
Therefore we hope that N. your servant
may be numbered among your blessed (high) priests
and inherit a crown and reward with all those
who have exercised faithfully this holy ministry.

And so, we join the powers of heaven
to celebrate with joy your eternal glory
in this, their ageless hymn of praise:

Holy . . .

---

* *For a deacon this line reads:*
to whom he committed ministries in his Church.

8. Funerals of Baptized Children

Grief and praise are juxtaposed as the duty of the Church in praying for children who die. The baptismal reference is not explicit in the Latin. However, it makes the sense and context of the preface clearer if it is included.

It is truly right and just, our duty and our salvation,
always, here and everywhere to give you thanks,
Lord, holy Father, almighty and eternal God,
through Jesus Christ our Lord.

Christ endows the Church, his bride,
with a tender love as Mother of all the living.
Hers is the grief of all who mourn their children;
hers also is the praise of your name
because these innocents have found salvation.
Great and wonderful, Lord God, is the mystery of our
    baptism;
for while the world grieves for children it has lost,
your Church rejoices that she has gained them for heaven.

In company with the angels,
they sing your praises in the presence of the Lamb.
Confident in their blessedness,
we join them to glorify your name
in this, their ageless hymn of praise:

Holy . . .

9. Funerals of Children who Die Before Baptism

This short preface is taken from that for the Anniversary of Several Dead, ii. Only the first three lines of the text are employed.

It is truly right and just, our duty and our salvation,
always, here and everywhere to give you thanks,
Lord, holy Father, almighty and eternal God,
through Jesus Christ our Lord.

Christ is the Saviour of the world,
the life of all, the resurrection of the dead.

And so, Lord God, with angels and all saints
we exult and glorify your holy name:

Holy . . .